In the name of Allah, the Most Beneficent, the Most Merciful

Ayatullah Jawadi Amuli, one of the great scholars of Islam, has a beautiful analogy pertaining to the stories in the Quran. He says *our grandmothers and mothers read us bedtime stories to put us to sleep, but Allah tells us stories in the Quran to wake us up from our sleep of heedlessness*.

Stories in the Quran and those of the Prophets and Imams are lessons sent from Allah to help guide us. When we read about different challenges the Prophet experienced throughout his life, we can learn to apply his lessons to our own lives. After in-depth studies, research, and discussions with scholars and educators, we have chosen these particular stories because we feel that they contain the most practical and applicable lessons for our daily lives.

In the following stories, you will see how even though the Prophet (s) had knowledge of the unseen and could perform miracles, he did not use them in his daily life. Like us, he patiently bore the challenges of life and made the best out of each situation.

Indeed, the Prophets and Imams are our true role models, or *uswa*, for us to aspire to be like. Though some stories may not directly apply to your life, there is still a lesson to learn, or a value to take away from each one— such as *tawakkul* (reliance), *sabr* (patience), *ikhlaas* (sincerity), and countless others!

I sincerely pray that we can all benefit from, and enjoy these stories. More importantly, I hope we can all act upon the lessons that they teach us. The Noble Prophet of Allah is a source of guidance and mercy for all of mankind, and insha'Allah these stories will help us all become better followers of our beloved Prophet and his family.

With Du'as,
Nabi R. Mir (Abidi)

Contents

CHAPTER 1

Kindness
is part of faith

Old or Young

There once lived an elderly, pious woman in the city of Medina, who wanted to enter jannah more than anything. She knew her time in this world was limited, so she focused her energy on becoming the best Muslim and servant of Allah that she could possibly be. Entering jannah was her heart's greatest desire, so she constantly made du'a to Allah to allow her to enter heaven. One day, she thought to herself, *If I ask the Prophet to make du'a on my behalf, Allah will surely grant me entrance into heaven!* She knew that Allah will always accept the du'as of His Prophet (s).

Excitedly, the woman set out to introduce herself to the Prophet (s). When she arrived, she greeted him warmly with salaam and asked, "O Noble Prophet of Allah! I want nothing more than to go to heaven. Are elderly people like myself welcome into heaven? O Prophet, will you kindly make du'a to Allah that I enter heaven?"

With a serious expression, the Prophet (s) greeted her back and told her simply, "There will be no elderly women in heaven."

When the woman heard these words, her heart sank and disappointment clouded her wrinkled face. *Oh no!* She thought with tears in her eyes, *This means I will never be among those will enter paradise!*

The Prophet (s) noticed the disappointed look on her face, so before the woman became too sad, he smiled and said, "Don't you remember Allah's words? He tells us in the Quran, 'We will turn the heavenly women into young, beautiful ladies.'" [1]

As she listened, the elderly woman realized that the Prophet (s) was joking, and immediately understood what he was trying to tell her. This verse means that each and every person in heaven will be young, even if they were old when they passed away. The Prophet (s) was reminding her that Allah restores youth and good health to every individual before he or she enters paradise. Her face brightened with joy as she realized that heaven was within her reach after all! She looked up at the Prophet (s), grinning from ear to ear. The Noble Prophet's (s) joke and wise reminder had filled her heart with hope. The pious woman happily returned home, feeling younger and better with every step she took!

---

1. Sūrat al-Wāqi'ah, Verses 35-38

Biḥār al-Anwār, Vol. 16, P. 29

Read to Succeed!

- The Prophet (s) even used humor as opportunities to teach. As narrated, we see that the Prophet (s) could teach someone about the many characteristics of heaven and familiarize them with a verse of the Holy Quran— all through a simple, but truthful, joke!

- The Prophet (s) was kind-hearted and had a calming presence. He and his companions would even joke with each other sometimes. He appreciated intelligent and friendly jokes, and was never bothered by humor that brought joy and laughter to people. As long as a joke was not offensive or hurtful, he smiled and appreciated them!

- Imam as-Sadiq (a) once asked his companion, Yunus Shaybani, "Do you joke with people?" Yunus replied, "Not often."
The Imam (a) replied, "It shouldn't be that way! Humor is part of good akhlaq, so long as it isn't sinful or hurtful to others. When you joke with others, you spread happiness. The Prophet (s) himself used jokes and light humor to bring others joy."

4

The Merciless Crowd

One day, while strolling through the city, the Noble Prophet (s) came across a crowd of people gathered on the road. Their laughter and buzzing excitement was clear, even from a distance. As the Prophet (s) drew closer, he saw what was making the crowd so excited—they were torturing a rooster! The Prophet (s) could hardly believe what he was seeing! The people of his city were being cruel to an animal, just for their own entertainment, and they seemed to be enjoying every horrible minute of it!

In the center of the crowd, the frail rooster jumped around in distress, clearly in pain. A loud croaking sound came from its dry throat, but no one showed any signs of mercy. Its feathers were scattered on the ground, and blood trickled steadily down its head. Still, not one person in the crowd seemed to care. Instead, they started to throw rocks at the rooster from every direction!

The rooster ran from side to side, desperately trying to dodge the flying rocks and escape. Soon, the rooster was too weak to even lift itself off the ground. The wounded animal's tired attempts to move only made the crowd laugh harder. The Prophet (s) watched this happen and became upset by their behavior .

He made his way through the crowd and stood in front of the rooster to shield it. The shower of rocks suddenly stopped, as everyone froze once they saw the Noble Prophet (s) standing right in front of them.

He scolded the ignorant and merciless crowd, and told them that their behavior was absolutely unacceptable. Hurting any creature, no matter how big or small, is not what Muslims do! Cruelty is *definitely* not a permissible way to have fun! The stern words of the Prophet (s) seemed to knock some sense into the crowd, and they hung their heads in shame. Realizing what they had done, they said sorry and began to leave.

The Prophet (s) was not against healthy forms of sports and entertainment, but all fun activities should be of a good and safe nature. Sometimes he participated in horse-racing competitions with his companions. Other times, when playing with children, he would pretend to be a horse and let them ride on his back. Through his example, we can see that Islam teaches us how to find healthy sources of fun and games. The Prophet (s) reminded the

Sunan Abī Dāwūd, Vol. 1, P. 592

crowd that there is a difference between healthy entertainment and unhealthy entertainment, the second form usually being at the *expense* of someone else.

We should not participate in any activity that is harmful to any person or creature, including ourselves!

Read to Succeed!

- Islam teaches us that we should divide our day into three parts:
  1. Taking care of our responsibilities, such as family, school or work.
  2. Worshipping Allah.
  3. Partaking in healthy entertainment.

- One of our responsibilities as Muslims is to encourage others to do good (*Amr bil Maruf*) and discourage them from evil *(Nahi Anil Munkar)*. When we see something harmful or cruel happening, it is our duty to recognize it and find a solution to it. If you can't solve the problem yourself, find someone who can. The Prophet (s) did not remain silent as he passed the crowd of people abusing the rooster. He immediately informed them that their actions were not permissible and did not align with the teachings of Islam.

- Kindness is an essential part of our faith. The Prophet (s) said, "Allah is kind, and He likes kind people." He also said, "Only the kind-hearted will enter paradise." Clearly, it is important for a Muslim to be kind and never cause harm to other people or animals.

- Even violence and cruelty in video games and movies should be avoided. After continuous exposure to violence and cruelty, our subconscious begins to accept it as normal, and we may start to think it is okay. That is why we should try to make sure all of our entertainment is healthy for our bodies as well as our souls.

Salman was a close companion of the Prophet (s). He converted to Islam after a long journey, and had left his family behind in Persia. This journey had been difficult and left him quite poor. What Salman lacked in wealth, however, he made up for in love and good character. He loved the Prophet (s) immensely, and the Prophet (s) returned this love as well.

One day, Salman went to visit the Noble Prophet (s) and received a warm welcome from him. When some of the wealthy guests noticed this, they became jealous of the attention Salman received from the Prophet (s).

They were angry to see the Prophet (s) give so much love and respect to a *poor* non-Arab man! These guests felt that only men like themselves, who were Arab, wealthy, and popular, deserved that kind of respect. One of the men loudly complained, "Who is this Persian man who has gained so much respect and honor among us? Why does the Prophet (s) show *him* so much love and respect? We are so much better than him!"

The Prophet (s) heard this and was displeased with their way of thinking. He did not want any of his followers to think or behave so arrogantly! To solve the issue, the Prophet (s) stood at the pulpit to address it.

He told them, "O my brothers! All human beings who have existed from the time of Prophet Adam (a) until now are equal, just as each seed in a pomegranate is equal. Each seed is similar in size, and tastes as sweet as the one that rests next to it! But, do you know what makes a person better than another? It is their *taqwa*, God-consciousness, and good deeds."

He then turned toward Salman and explained, "Because of Salman's high level of taqwa, he is from us, the Ahlul Bayt!"

Surely, only Allah can decide what elevates one person over another. Take the example of a comb. Have you ever noticed how each of the thin teeth that make up a comb are the same length? They're entirely equal, and no one part works better than another! In the same way, Arabs are not superior to non-Arabs, white people are not superior to people of color, and wealthy people are not superior to poor people! The only thing that elevates one person above another is the way they follow Allah's commands.

Read To Succeed!

- Although the Prophet (s) was sent to Arabia, Allah intended his message to be for *all* people and for *all* times. Islam is a *universal* religion, and it is not limited to just one time or place. That is why Salman, Suhayb, and Bilal all accepted the religion of Islam and became companions of the Prophet (s), even though they were from different regions like Persia, Rome, and Africa.

- Being considered as the family of the Prophet (s) is not limited to Sayyids only. This story shows that anyone can be considered part of the Ahlul Bayt (a) by increasing their faith and following the Prophet's (s) example.

- Our ahadith tell us that other companions, such as Abu Dhar, Jabir, Miqdad, and Ammar, are also part of the Ahlul Bayt (a). This is because although they were not related to him, their actions were in line with his teachings, and their behavior elevated their status!

- The Ahlul Bayt (a) loved and respected Salman so much that instead of saying Salman al-Farsi, they would say Salman al-Muhammadi. Once, a man said to Imam as-Sadiq (a), "You speak often of Salman al-Farsi." The Imam replied, "Don't refer to him as Salman al-Farsi; call him Salman-al-Muhammadi."

The Thirsty Kitten

Once, a thirsty kitten wandered through the winding streets of Medina. Many hours had passed since she last drank a sip of water, and this made her tongue very dry. It was a really hot and sunny day, and the heat made her even thirstier! The kitten was tired, but knew she had to look for water.

She searched the usual places for water, but today, there was none to be found! The poor kitten went through many backyards and alleyways, but she couldn't find a single drop of water to drink.

Eventually, after much wandering, the kitten found herself in the Prophet's (s) yard. The Prophet (s) was holding a bowl of water, ready to perform wudhu. The kitten's gaze immediately fell upon the bowl in his hands, and her eyes lit up. She had found water at last! She wanted to leap forward and quench her thirst with the cold, refreshing water, but she stayed where she was. The bowl was out of her reach!

The sight of the kitten caught the Prophet (s) by surprise. One look at the little kitten made it clear to the Prophet (s) that she was thirsty and tired. He felt sorry for the kitten, and knew he had to help.

The Prophet (s) taught his companions that giving water to the thirsty, even animals, is an action that Allah will reward. Without hesitating, he bent down and placed the water bowl directly in front of the kitten. The kitten watched the Prophet (s) do this, and meowed with happiness. She was so glad he placed the water within her reach!

She trotted toward the bowl and lapped the water up quickly and happily. When she had drank enough to quench her thirst, she lifted her head from the bowl with much more energy than before.

She looked at the Prophet (s) with immense gratitude, and the Prophet (s) smiled down at her. He watched as she wandered back to the streets of Medina with a new bounce in her step. Truly, the Prophet (s) was sent as a mercy to all of Allah's creations, both humans and animals!

Read to Succeed!

⚜ All living things need water to survive and lack of water puts their lives at risk. There is a divine reward for offering water to any person or creature that is thirsty. Imam al-Baqir (a) said, "Allah likes it when we quench a person's thirst. Whoever gives water to a thirsty person, Allah will shade this person with His mercy."

⚜ There once was a man who everyone disliked because he sinned often. One day, he saw a thirsty dog. The man felt sorry for the dog and, noticing a well nearby, walked towards it to get water. He saw that there was no rope to draw the water up; only a bucket on the ground. He took off his shirt and used it as a rope, attaching the bucket to one end and holding the other end in his hands. He lowered the bucket into the well and soon, he drew out water! The man took the water to the thirsty dog, who lapped it up with gratitude. It pleased Allah to see the man's good deed and He said to the Prophet (s), "I am happy with this man for showing kindness to one of My creatures. I have forgiven his sins." When the Prophet (s) gave this man the good news, he was thrilled. He asked for forgiveness for his past sins and worked to become a more virtuous man.

Charity Wards Off Misfortune

One day, a disbeliever who always insulted and bothered the Prophet (s) passed by him on the street. Instead of greeting the Prophet (s) by saying *"Assalaamu Alaykum,"* which means "peace be upon you," the man said, "*Assaam Alaykum,*" which means "death be upon you." The companions of the Prophet (s) heard these cruel words and were extremely upset.

The Prophet (s) calmly told them, "Every bad action has a consequence. Have faith in Allah's justice! If this man continues to behave cruelly and sin in this way, surely a snake will bite him today."

The man walked past and went on to collect firewood. Meanwhile, the companions lingered to see when the Prophet's (s) prediction would come true. After some time, the man returned with a sack full of firewood flung over his shoulder. He showed no signs of pain or discomfort from being bitten by a snake.

The companions of the Prophet (s) were surprised. They knew the Prophet (s) always told the truth, so they wondered how it was possible that this man was still alive!

The Prophet (s) saw that his companions were confused. To show them what had happened, he asked the man to put his load of firewood down for a moment. The man did as he was asked, and the companions began to inspect the firewood. To their surprise, they saw a black snake curled up on one of the pieces of wood! They knew it was the same snake that was supposed to punish him for insulting Allah's Prophet (s)! But why didn't it bite him?!

The Prophet (s) asked the man, "What did you do today?"

The man answered, "I went out to collect firewood and packed two sandwiches for the trip. I ate one of them on the way and was saving the second one for later. On my way to the woods, I came across a hungry man and decided he needed the other sandwich more than I did, so I gave it to him and carried on with my day."

The Prophet (s) smiled with understanding. He turned to his companions and said, "Do you see? This single good deed saved him from the misfortune that was originally meant to come his way." That day, the companions learned that charity and kindness can ward off the greatest of misfortunes, including death!

Read to Succeed!

- Allah has designed the world so that everybody will experience some type of consequences for their actions, good or bad, in this world. There will certainly be rewards and punishments in the afterlife, but people can also see the effects of their actions right here, on Earth, as well!

- Charity should be a regular part of our lives. The Prophet (s) stressed the importance of charity by advising us:
  - "Charity is rewarded tenfold."
  - "Charity takes away punishment."
  - "When a person extends his hand to give charity, Allah will be pleased with this person and Allah forgives whomever He is pleased with."
  - "Charity wards off evil."
  - "Charity increases one's sustenance. So, give in charity, and Allah will be merciful toward you."

- A man came to Imam al-Kadhim (a) and asked, "I am sick, and my family members are all ill as well. What should I do?" The Imam answered, "Cure them by giving charity. Nothing is accepted by Allah as quickly as an act of charity. For the sick, there is no medicine better than charity!" Of course, we must go to the doctor and take our medicine too!

- Charity does not just involve money! Some of the best forms of charity are performing good deeds. Think about what daily acts of charity you can do at home, school, or the masjid!

12

Noble Forgiveness

Anas was a boy who lived in Medina and loved the Noble Prophet (s) very much. Sometimes Anas would visit the Prophet (s) and help him with chores and errands. If the Prophet (s) was busy, Anas would help him by going to the market and getting groceries for the Prophet (s), or delivering messages to his companions.

One day, Prophet Muhammad (s) was fasting and Anas was with him at his house. The Prophet (s) left the house just an hour before Maghrib time. When Maghrib came, it was time to break the fast, and Anas had prepared a simple iftaar for the Prophet (s). Anas waited for him to return, but there was no sign of the Prophet (s)! He waited a little while longer, but still, the Prophet (s) did not return.

Anas thought that perhaps one of the Prophet's (s) companions invited him for iftaar. If the Prophet (s) was out for dinner somewhere else, Anas figured it would be okay if he went ahead and ate the meal he prepared himself! Anas then happily ate the iftaar, certain that the Prophet (s) had eaten elsewhere.

Soon after, the Noble Prophet (s) finally returned home with some of his companions. Anas greeted them and asked one of the companions, "Was the Prophet (s) invited to one of your homes for iftaar? Has he eaten something?" He replied, "No, he hasn't eaten anything yet."

Anas' face turned pale as he realized what a huge mistake he had made. If the Prophet (s) knew what happened, Anas would feel so embarrassed! He knew the Prophet (s) was kind and would forgive him, but knowing that did not make Anas feel any less ashamed.

The Prophet (s) soon realized what had happened. He saw empty plates and no food on the table, which could only mean that there was none left for him. "I don't feel hungry tonight" the Prophet (s) said, and he went to bed. Anas was amazed. The Prophet (s) went to bed on an empty stomach, just so that Anas would not be embarrassed!

Amazingly, the Prophet (s) never once mentioned that night's iftaar to Anas. Anas was so grateful the Prophet (s) showed him this kindness that his love for him grew even more. Islam teaches us to cover the mistakes or sins of others, rather than expose them. We should all strive to be as kind and forgiving as our beloved Prophet (s)!

Read to Succeed!

- Some people react with anger and complain about the slightest mistake made by others. True believers, however, overlook others' faults and do not easily become upset. In this anecdote, the Prophet (s), did not mention the iftaar so that Anas would not feel embarrassed. Instead, he acted as though nothing had happened!

- We can see through this anecdote that love and patience teaches better than anger and raised voices.
  Try this: find a partner and role play being forgiving and kind instead of getting upset and yelling.

- The Noble Prophet (s) was lenient and forgiving, and advised others to be likewise. He said, "The most sensible of all people is the sort who is lenient and overlooks others' mistakes. Allah the Almighty Himself is lenient and kind and likes leniency and kindness in all matters. My Lord has ordered me to be kind Just as He has ordered me to perform wajib acts. Leniency with people is half of faith. Between two friends, he who is softer and lenient toward others is more loved by Allah."

Feeding a Sheep

The Prophet (s) and his friends were eating dates. He collected the pits that were left on the ground by them, but nobody was sure why the Prophet (s) did this. Some people guessed that perhaps he wanted to plant the pits.

There were some sheep grazing nearby, munching on grass and walking all over a wide field. One of the sheep passed by the Prophet (s). He opened and stretched his hand toward the sheep, inviting it to come forward and eat the pits. The sheep turned its head toward the Prophet's (s) hand and happily started eating!

The Prophet (s) continued to feed the sheep. The sheep enjoyed every single one and left when there were no more.

In this way, the Prophet (s) showed his friends how one can even use things we think are insignificant, such as date pits, to please the creatures of Allah!

Read to Succeed!

- Here are some additional stories about the Prophet's kindness to animals:

  A man came to the Noble Prophet (s) to ask for financial help. The Prophet (s) ordered for him to be given some camels and then addressed him, "When you reach home, ask your family to give the camels proper food. Likewise, ask them them to clip their nails so that they do not hurt the animals' udders while milking them."

- The Prophet (s) saw a man milking a sheep and said to him, "Make sure to leave some milk for the sheep's lamb to drink."

- In the past, people used to tattoo animals by placing a mark or number with a smoldering iron on their backs. The sign was usually made on their backs and not faces, so as to avoid torturing the animal. Once the Noble Prophet (s) saw a donkey with a tattoo on its face. The Noble Prophet (s) was very disturbed by the sight and said: "Haven't you heard that I am unhappy with those who make signs on or whip animals' faces?"

Helping Haleemah

The Noble Prophet (s) could never forget the kindness of Haleemah, the woman who had nursed and looked after him as a child. In those times, the people of Mecca often handed over their babies to families who lived outside the city because those regions were safer for children. There, the children could grow up away from dangerous diseases and other issues.

When the Noble Prophet (s) was born, he was handed over to Haleemah for the same reason. She was from the tribe of Bani Sa'ad, who all lived outside Mecca. Women of that tribe were known to be great nurses, so everyone knew that Muhammad (s) would be in good hands.

Haleemah nursed him for two years and looked after him until he was 5. Growing up, Prophet Muhammad (s) never took her kindness and care for granted. He respected her immensely, and loved her like his own mother. In fact, he used to say to people, "Haleemah is also my mother."

The years passed, and soon, the Noble Prophet (s) had blossomed into a young man and married Hadhrat Khadijah (a). During those years, a drought hit the surrounding areas of Mecca. Haleemah's tribe suffered badly because of this drought! They lost their herd as a result, and soon the people of Bani Sa'ad had nothing left to eat.

Haleemah decided to visit the Prophet (s) in Mecca and ask him to help her people. On seeing her, the Noble Prophet (s) treated her with great respect, and attentively listened to everything she said. It was clear to him that she was going through a difficult time and needed help.

After hearing her explanation of the problem, he went to discuss the situation with his wife, Khadijah (a). She was kind and a successful, wealthy business woman, so the Prophet (s) knew she would be capable of helping Haleemah and her tribe.

After speaking with Khadijah (a), the Prophet (s) returned to Haleemah with forty sheep and camels. Haleemah was overjoyed at their generosity, and returned home relieved and grateful. Forty sheep and camels were plenty for the people of her tribe. They could use the herd for both milk and meat throughout the drought!

Biḥār al-Anwār, Vol. 15, P. 401

With this great act of generosity, Prophet Muhammad (s) demonstrated that he could never forget Haleemah's role in his childhood, and that no favor could ever truly repay her for her love and warmth!

Read to Succeed!

⚙ In this story, we see an example of the Messenger of Allah (s) thanking Haleemah for all she did for him in his childhood. Gratitude to those who have been good to us is very important.

⚙ Following the conquest of Mecca, a relative of Haleemah from the tribe of Bani Sa'ad visited the Noble Prophet (s) with a gift. The Noble Prophet (s) accepted her gift and enquired about Haleemah. She said, "She has passed away." Tears welled up in the Noble Prophet's (s) eyes. It was clear that he had not forgotten her, and still loved her dearly.

⚙ Khadijah played a crucial role in the spread of Islam. She was the first woman to embrace Islam and, thereafter, handed all her wealth and belongings to our dear Prophet (s) for the sake of Islam. Her contribution was unforgettable for the Noble Prophet (s). He used to say, "She believed in me when all others disbelieved, she confirmed my message when others rejected it, and when others drove me away, she protected me."

It Isn't Your Turn

One of the duties of the Noble Prophet (s) was answering the many questions of the believers. He usually did this at home or at the masjid. Those who had questions came to him at one of these locations and asked whatever they wanted to know, one by one. Since there were many people with important questions, they all took turns, and whoever arrived first, asked his question first!

The Noble Prophet (s) did not like for anyone to ask a question out of turn. The Muslims learned from his example that it was important to respect other people's turns.

One day, an Ansaar (inhabitant of Medina) came to the Prophet (s) to ask a question. Right after him, a man from the tribe of Thaqeef came to do the same. He, too, had a question. He said to the Noble Prophet (s), "O Prophet of Allah! I need to ask you something."

The Messenger of Allah (s) replied, "Of course you can, but this Muslim brother of yours arrived earlier. InshaAllah, you can go after him."

The Prophet (s) wanted to remind the Thaqeefi brother to respect the Ansaar man's turn. The Prophet (s) was about to start answering the Ansaar's question when the Thaqeefi politely said, "O Prophet (s) of Allah! I have to go on a journey, so I am in a hurry." The Ansaar kindly said, "O Messenger! Since he is in a hurry, I give him my turn."

With the consent of the Ansaar man, the Noble Prophet (s) accepted the Thaqeefi's question first.

Read to Succeed!

- Those who cut in line are compared to thieves. They steal people's time and turns instead of their money, and that is just as bad!

- If someone is truly in a hurry it is highly recommended to give up your turn for that person. While taking another person's turn isn't allowed, exchanging it through mutual consent is definitely a good way to do it!

Helping Sayyidah Fatimah (a)

One day, the Noble Prophet (s) went to visit Imam Ali (a) and Sayyidah Fatimah (a), his daughter and son-in-law, who he loved more than anything.

The Prophet (s) entered their home, greeted them, and saw them both hard at work. They were grinding barley and wheat with a grinding stone to make flour.

Working with a grinding stone was difficult and tiring, so the Noble Prophet (s) asked, "Which one of you is more tired?" Ali (a) didn't wait for Fatimah (a) to answer. He said, "O Prophet of Allah, my wife Fatimah (a) is more tired."

The Noble Prophet (s) looked at Fatimah (a) and said, "My daughter, please let me take your place." Fatimah (a) stood up and moved aside. The Prophet (s) then sat down and began to continue her work! SubhaanAllah, the Noble Prophet (s) was so humble! He had so much love for Imam Ali (a) and Sayyidah Fatimah (a)!

Read to Succeed!

⚙ Sayyidah Fatimah (a) and Imam Ali (a) divided chores between each other. Outside chores were Imam Ali's (a) responsibility and Sayyidah Fatimah (a) did the housework. However, Imam Ali (a) always helped his wife at home too.

⚙ Sayyidah Fatimah (a) grinded wheat and did household chores like the rest of the women. She baked bread, washed clothes, and swept the house. She lived simply and never thought she deserved better because she was the daughter of the Prophet (s).

⚙ The Noble Prophet (s) said regarding Sayyidah Fatimah (a):

- Fatimah is a part of me. She is the fruit of my heart and light of my eyes.
- Fatimah is the leader of the women of the worlds.
- Whoever pleases Fatimah pleases me, and whoever hurts her hurts me.
- Fatimah is dearest to me amongst all.
- Whenever I feel like smelling paradise, I smell my daughter Fatimah.

The Man Who Sat Alone

Once, the Prophet's (s) companions were sitting together eating. Suddenly, they were joined by a man who had all sorts of unpleasant patches on his face. The man he sat next to took one look at his face and stood up in disgust to sit elsewhere. No one wanted to sit near him! Everyone in his presence got up to leave, one by one.

The poor man was heartbroken; he did not expect this kind of reaction from his fellow Muslim brothers, nor did he think that Muslims would treat him so horribly just because he looked different from them. The man was deeply hurt, and so overwhelmed that he did not know what to do or where to go.

Prophet Muhammad (s) was seated nearby, and saw how the Muslims were treating this man. When he saw that not a single person sat with the man, he himself went and sat next to him. When the man looked up and saw the Prophet (s) sitting beside him, he was overcome with joy and gratitude. The Prophet (s) smiled at him, and began a pleasant conversation with him to help him feel less lonely.

Everyone who had gotten up saw the Prophet (s) do this, and felt deeply ashamed for their actions. As they saw the Prophet (s) laughing and chatting with the man, they realized he was no different from anyone else. Without being told to, one by one they each returned to sit in the man's company.

With this simple act of humanity, the Noble Prophet (s) showed his companions that no one has the right to be unkind to anyone just because they look different. Allah created people in all different shapes, sizes, and colors. Some people may look different, maybe because they had an accident that resulted in a disability or scar, or because they were born with a birthmark or unique feature.

No one should be treated differently because of something they cannot control, like their appearance! Instead of shunning someone who looks different, we should aim to be like the Prophet (s) and celebrate the unique qualities that Allah blessed them with. After all, it is not appearance that elevates one person over another, but the goodness of their actions.

Biḥār al-Anwār, Vol. 73, P. 206

Read to Succeed!

⚙ Once Imam al-Kadhim (a) greeted a man with strange features who sat down next to him to talk. Some of the Imam's (a) companions who were walking by noticed, and wondered why the Imam was conversing warmly with such a person. The Imam reminded them, "He, too, is a servant of Allah, and according to the Quran, our brother in faith!"

⚙ One day, during his journey to Marv, Imam ar-Ridha (a) laid out a cloth and began serving food. He invited everyone, even the servants, to eat with him and his companions. One of his travelling companions requested, "O Imam, if you allow it, could we serve the workers elsewhere?" The Imam said, "No. We all have the same God, and we are all children of Prophet Adam and Hawwa. Everyone's reward and punishment in the hereafter is based on their deeds here, and everyone should be treated equally."

Freedom, At Last!

A camel once approached Prophet Muhammad (s) and started talking to him. The Prophet (s), who understood the language of all animals, could tell that the camel was unhappy. The camel complained to the Prophet (s) that his master was unjust, and provided very little food while expecting him to carry heavy loads.

The Noble Prophet (s) listened to the camel attentively, then turned to his companion, Jabir. He said, "O Jabir, go with this camel. He will guide you to his owner. When you find his master, bring him to see me."

Jabir followed the camel to the tribe of Bani Hanzhalah, where the camel easily located his master. After confirming with other people that this was the camel's master, Jabir led the man back to the Noble Prophet (s).

When they arrived, Prophet Muhammad (s) greeted the camel's master. He said to him, "Your camel tells me that you give him little food and overwork him."

The camel's owner responded, "O Prophet, it is true, but I did this only for two days! My camel was being disobedient, so I had no choice but to punish him. It will not happen again!"

It was clear from the master's tone that he did not regularly mistreat his camel, and wouldn't punish him that way again. The Prophet (s) was relieved to know that the camel was no longer in danger of being mistreated.

The Prophet (s) turned to the camel and said, "Now that this matter is settled, go back with your master," and handed over the animal to the man. The animal was comforted and began to walk home with his master.

The Prophet's (s) concerns for the animal deeply touched the owner's heart. He was so impressed to see that the Prophet's (s) akhlaq extended even to animals, that he decided to free the camel out of respect! The owner said to the Prophet (s), "I set this camel free for your sake, O Messenger of Allah! If you can care this much for an animal, the least I can do is free him! No one will ever mount him again, or burden him with any load."

Biḥār al-Anwār, Vol. 17, P. 417

From that day onwards, the camel lived freely in Medina. People who saw him would often point him out and say, "Look! This is the camel that was freed because of the Prophet of Allah!"

Read to Succeed!

⚙ Animals are creatures of Allah, and people who keep them should always take good care of them. Animals in your care should never go hungry or thirsty! Once, the Prophet (s) saw a hungry camel and was upset to see it neglected. He reminded his companions, "Remember Allah, and take care of these animals! They cannot speak and tell you what they need, so you must be extra careful!"

⚙ Some people try to take care of pets, but don't have the time, or prioritize other tasks instead. This kind of neglect is also oppression! One day, as the Prophet (s) was walking to the masjid, he saw a camel whose legs had been tied up to keep him from wandering away. It was clear from the camel's face that he was hungry, so the Prophet (s) looked around for its master. Once he found the man who owned the camel, he gently reminded him of his duties. "Brother, remember Allah, and do your best to take good care of the animals you are responsible for! You should feed him, but if you cannot, perhaps it would be best to free him."

Loving Your Mother

The Noble Prophet (s) endured many losses throughout his life. His father, Abdullah, died before Prophet Muhammad (s) was even born. When he was six years old, his mother Aminah also passed away.

When he was eight years old, his grandfather, Abdul Muttalib passed away. From then on, his uncle Abu Talib became his guardian, and the Prophet (s) was raised in his house.

The Prophet (s) had a hard life, and all of these losses brought him much sadness. Despite all of this, he never gave up and continued to live the best life he could. It is okay to be sad or emotional, as long as our feelings do not stop us from fulfilling our responsibilities.

When the Prophet (s) was 25, he married Khadijah (a), and then at 40 he was appointed as a Prophet. He lived in Mecca until he was 53 years old, and worked to spread the message of Islam. He then left for Medina and established an Islamic government there.

No matter how old he was or where he lived, he never forgot his mother. Once, when he was 58, he visited his mother's grave in Abwah. As the Noble Prophet (s) lovingly cleaned his mother's gravestone, his eyes filled with tears and he cried for some time. He missed her immensely, and could not contain his sadness in that moment.

His tears seemed strange to his friends. They wondered why a 58 year old man would cry at his mother's grave. When they asked him why he was crying, he responded, "I was missing my mother and that made me cry."

The Prophet (s) taught us in that moment just how important our mothers are. We should love and respect them even after they are gone, and take good care of their graves, just as we take care of them while they are still in our lives!

Biḥār al-Anwār, Vol. 15, P. 162

Read to Succeed!

🌸 From this story, we can learn that it is not only allowed, but important to visit the graves of our loved ones. Just as we visit the graves of loved ones, we should visit the shrines and harams of the Prophets and Imams! Some people object to visiting shrines of the Noble Prophet (s) and his holy family, but the Prophet (s) himself not only visited his mother's grave, but also cried by her grave!

🌸 An Arab woman converted to Islam, while her mother remained a disbeliever. She came to the Prophet (s) and asked, "O Prophet of God! I visited my mother and realized that she was still an infidel. Should I continue to be kind to her?" "Yes," he answered. "You must still be kind to her because she is still your mother."

CHAPTER 2

Remembering Allah & His Lessons

The Hungry Man

After a long, hard day of work, a man was walking toward Masjid al-Nabi when he felt his stomach growl from hunger. Tired from his long day, the man was eager to eat. When he reached the masjid, he pulled his lunch out of his bag, unwrapped his sandwich, and quickly began to devour it, as though he hadn't eaten in days! As he munched through this delicious and hard-earned meal, he felt more and more satisfied with every bite. He opened his mouth, ready to take the final bite, when he suddenly stopped, his mouth hanging open. His eyes widened as he realized that he had forgotten the most important step before eating!

Oh no! I forgot to thank Allah for this great meal that He blessed me with! he thought to himself regretfully, as he had tried to make a habit of beginning every meal with the words:

بِسِمِ اللّٰهِ الرَّحْمٰنِ الرَّحِيمِ

With the name of Allah, the Most Kind, the Most Merciful.

However, he was so hungry that he completely forgot to begin his meal with these blessed words! By the time he remembered to say Bismillah, he only had one bite left of his food. Before taking that last bite, he declared, "Bismillah—for my first bite, last bite, and all the bites I forgot in between!"

This happened not far from where Prophet Muhammad (s) was sitting with some of his companions. The companions had noticed that the man had forgotten to say Bismillah and drew the Prophet's (s) attention to his mistake.

After the man remembered to say Bismillah, the Prophet (s) smiled, turned to his companions, and explained, "When this man forgot to say Bismillah, Shaytaan became his companion and shared every bite of his meal with him. But as soon as he remembered Allah, Shaytaan went away!" With this lesson, the Prophet (s) showed his companions that even if you say it at the very last minute, just before your last bite, saying Bismillah is still extremely important!

Sunan Abī Dāwūd, Vol. 1, P. 592

Read to Succeed!

- In Islam it is highly recommended to begin every action by saying the words "Bismillahir Rahmanir Raheem." Imam as-Sadiq (a) said, "Do not ever abandon the habit of saying Bismillahir Rahmanir Raheem."

- In another hadith, the Prophet (s) said, "Any important activity that does not begin with Bismillah can not reach its full potential for success!"

- Imam as-Sadiq (a) has also said, "Sometimes our Shi'a begin without saying Bismillahir Rahmaanir Raheem. When this happens, Allah tests them with difficulties to help them remember to praise Him, be thankful, and return their attention toward Him."

- Allah has made plenty of food available so we can satisfy our hunger, nourish our bodies, help others, and worship Him. When we say Bismillah, we are thanking Allah and showing our appreciation for His blessings in the best way possible.

- Bismillah isn't just meant to thank Allah, it is also about remembering Allah in each and every thing we do. Remembering Allah before doing something will help you stop and think: will this action please Allah?

- Some actions we should begin with Bismillah include:
  - getting dressed
  - entering or leaving the home
  - going to sleep and waking up
  - going to school and completing assignments
  - entering a vehicle (car, train, bus, plane, etc.)

The Most Merciful

One day, a man came to visit the Noble Prophet (s), carrying his young child in his arms. The father cradled the child close to his chest, and his protectiveness made it clear to the Prophet (s) just how much he loved his child.

This warm and loving expression of a father's love for his child reminded the Prophet (s) of Allah's love for His creations. The Prophet (s) used this opportunity to remind the loving father about Allah's love for him, as well as the love the Almighty had placed in his heart for his child.

He asked the father, "Do you love this child of yours?" The father replied, "Yes, O Prophet of Allah, I do!" The Prophet (s) then explained, "The love and mercy that Allah has for you extends far beyond the love and mercy you have for your child. Allah is the *Most* Merciful!"

The man understood the words of the Prophet (s) clearly— just as his hands wrapped around his child, Allah's infinite love and mercy is like a warm cloak that surrounds all of His creation. SubhaanAllah!

Allah is undoubtedly the Most Kind and Merciful. All acts of kindness, love, and mercy that are seen in this world come from His kindness. It is Allah who puts the love of a child into the hearts of his or her parents. The original source of all love and mercy in the world is Allah. Signs of Allah's love are visible everywhere we turn, and no one loves us like Allah does. His love is unlimited! It is Allah who gave us families and friends, and it is He who provides us with a variety of delicious food. All good things in our lives are blessings from Him! It is Allah who made the sun a source of warmth and light, and Allah who sent the Prophets and Imams to guide mankind. Is there anyone more Merciful to us than Allah? Certainly not!

Biḥār al-Anwār, Vol. 22, P. 348

Read to Succeed!

- We all know how selfless and kind parents are, and that their hearts are full of love for their children. They want the best for them and strive to ensure their success and happiness. They do everything in their power to ensure their children have a good life, both in this world and the hereafter. Have you ever wondered who planted all that love, care, and kindness in their hearts? Consider this: a parent's love is like a drop of water compared to the ocean of love that Allah has for His creation.

- Once, the Prophet (s) was sitting in the masjid. A desert nomad entered and said,"O Allah, forgive Muhammad and me, and do not forgive anyone else." He said this under the mistaken belief that Allah's mercy was limited and available to only a few special people. The nomad incorrectly thought the more Allah bestows His mercy upon the people, the less mercy Allah would have for him in particular! In response to his du'a, the Prophet (s) said, "You have underestimated Allah's vast mercy!"

Work Hard, Pray Hard

One day, Angel Jibraeel came down to Earth and revealed the second and third verses of Surah Talaq to the Prophet (s). In this surah, Allah says: "He who believes in Allah and the Last Day (and) fears the punishment of Allah, Allah will make a way out for him, and provide him with sustenance from where he least expects it. Allah is enough for one who relies on Him."

The Prophet (s) listened to these verses and then went to repeat them to the Muslims. These verses mean that Allah will always take care of our needs in this world, as long as we believe in Him and trust Him. Even when we feel helpless or stuck, Allah will find a solution because nothing is impossible for Allah!

Some people, however, did not understand what these verses meant. They thought that if they believed in Allah and prayed to Him all day long, He would automatically provide them with food and shelter. They assumed that Allah was telling them that they no longer had to work hard! So, these people stopped going to work. Instead, they decided to stay home and pray, certain that Allah would take care of everything else.

From sunrise to sunset, they would pass the entire day in prayer. When friends asked them why they stopped working, they simply recited the two verses of Surah Talaq as an explanation before going back to their prayers.

When the Prophet (s) learned of these people who prayed but no longer worked, he asked to talk to them. When they arrived, the Prophet asked, "Why have you stopped working? Is there a reason you have put aside your jobs?"

One person replied, "O Prophet, we are following the guidance of the Quran! The verses you revealed to us promise that Allah will provide pure and pious believers with sustenance. We are trying to be pious by praying all day long! Our prayers guarantee that Allah will give us what we need so we don't need to work anymore!"

The Prophet (s) realized that these people did not understand the true meaning of these verses. He knew he had to clarify the meaning for them. He explained to them, "If someone stops working and does not try to fulfill his responsibilities, his du'as will not be accepted."

Biḥār al-Anwār, Vol. 22, P. 121, Vol. 7, P. 281

Of course, making du'a and having imaan are prerequisites to success! We have to trust that Allah alone will reward us for our hard work. But praying without working hard is not what Allah wants from us! Relying on Allah means working hard to earn sustenance, *then* leaving the rest to Allah.

The people realized their mistake and quickly went back to their normal routines. They finally understood that working hard is a form of worship, just like praying or fasting.

Consider it this way: if you don't go to school, how will you ever be able to read and write? If you do not travel to different lands, how can you expect to see their natural beauty? In order to gain something, you must be willing to put in the effort! Similarly, praying without working toward your goal will have no effect!

Read to Succeed!

- Du'as (also called supplicating) is very important. Du'a is how we speak to Allah and develop a close relationship with Him. Allah loves those who speak and make du'a to Him often. Prophet Muhammad (S) has said, "There is nothing dearer to Allah than supplicating to Him." Imam as-Sadiq (A) said, "Make du'a often, because nothing brings you closer to Allah like du'a." However, we must remember that du'a is not a replacement for hard work. We must work hard *and* pray hard.

- We should be careful when trying to interpret verses from the Holy Quran by ourselves! We should not jump to conclusions before we have enough knowledge about a subject. In this story, a group of people misinterpreted the verses of the Quran due to their limited understanding. Be careful so that you don't make the same mistake!

- According to Islam, working hard to earn a living in an honest and halal way is itself *ibadaah* (a form of worship). We should not think that praying and fasting are the only ways of worship. The Prophet (s) has said, "Worship has seventy parts, the best of which is to earn a lawful living."

- Prophet Dawood (a) said to a shoemaker, "Work and live off your own earnings because Allah loves those who work for their livelihood, and does not like those who live off others."

The Small Becomes Significant

Once, the Prophet (s) and his companions had been traveling for a long time, and became completely exhausted. When the companions grew hungry, they found a good place to rest and dismounted from their horses. The Noble Prophet (s) asked everyone to look for firewood, so they could cook their food. Everyone in the group set out to search for firewood.

One by one, they all came back empty-handed and complained, "This place is a desert! It is dry and empty, and there is no firewood to be found!" The companions were right— this land wasn't like Medina, where firewood was readily available. Still, the Prophet encouraged them to go out again and bring back whatever wood they could get their hands on.

The companions dispersed again, knowing that the Prophet (s) knew best. This time, they set out in every direction and looked even more carefully. There were no large branches, but they managed to find small twigs jutting from the sand. Some were as small as match sticks! They picked them up, figuring they could add them to the fire. They collected as much as they could and returned to the Prophet (s). Some had collected only a handful of sticks, and others had even less than that. All of them combined their tiny piles, and when they had gathered everything together, they were shocked to see the pile of wood was large enough to cook their meal!

The Prophet (s) wanted to teach them an important lesson through this. He gathered the companions and said, "I want you to learn something from your experience today. Just as these small twigs became a large, significant pile when collected, small actions become significant when they are added together.

The companions learned an important lesson that day: small sins should not be taken lightly or dismissed, because they can easily grow and gather together, becoming significant over time. On the other hand, they should do plenty of good deeds, no matter how small they seem, because every small deed counts and contributes to the larger picture!

Read to Succeed!

- Life is full of lessons and experiences that we can benefit from. From this narration, we see that many small sticks gathered together can make a large, useful pile. Think about the trash cans at school. You might only put in one piece of trash, but by the end of the day, the can will be overflowing with garbage! Have you ever seen your laundry pile grow to an uncontrollable size when you forgot to wash your clothes regularly?

- The Prophet never missed any opportunity to teach his companions lessons through ordinary, daily experiences. Even in the midst of a difficult journey in a dry and hot desert, the Prophet was able to teach them an important life lesson. We should never take our mistakes lightly, no matter how small they seem, because if we fail to repent and fix them, they will pile up and become significant!

Biḥār al-Anwār, Vol. 73, P. 367

The Wise Old Lady

In the olden days, many people lived and worked on farms where they could grow their own crops. Animals served many different purposes, such as providing transportation, food, and milk to drink. Some animals were useful for their wool, which was an excellent resource used to make clothes. The wool is spun into yarn, which then gets woven into clothes!

On one particular farm, there lived an old lady who made a living by spinning wool into yarn to make clothes. She would comb the freshly sheared wool, then use a spinning wheel to turn the individual strands of wool into thick, strong yarn. In order to work properly, the spinning wheel needed a person to feed the wool into it and keep it spinning. Once the yarn was completely spun, people could then use it to create fabric for clothes or blankets.

One day, Prophet Muhammad (s) was passing by this farm and saw the old lady sitting outside and spinning yarn. As he approached her, he said salaam and asked her how she was doing. She replied, "Wa alaikum as salaam, O Prophet! I am well, alhamdulillah! Right now, I am working on spinning this wool."

They spoke for a few minutes and the Prophet (s) thanked her for all of her hard work. The old woman was thrilled to hear the Prophet's (s) kind words. Soon, the conversation turned to Allah and His many blessings! The Prophet (s) was curious to learn about the old woman's strong faith, so he asked her an interesting question.

"How do you know Allah exists?" the Prophet (s) asked her. The old lady stopped spinning for a moment, and looked up at him thoughtfully.

After thinking quietly, she said, "This simple spinning wheel needs someone to spin it for it to work properly. If I stop pushing it for even a second, it slows down and then stops spinning altogether. This world is much larger and more complicated than a spinning wheel! Just as my hand keeps the wheel spinning, surely there is an All-Powerful force, a Creator, who oversees the world and keeps it spinning!"

Biḥār al-Anwār, Vol. 69, P. 135

The Prophet (s) was impressed by the woman's intelligent response to his question, and remarked that everyone should try to strengthen their faith and *imaan* through deep reflection and understanding (called *ma'rifah*), just like this old woman did!

Read to Succeed!

⚙ One of the best ways to know Allah and increase our faith in Him is to look for signs of His existence around us. Many verses of the Quran tell us to spend time thinking about natural marvels so we can come to know Allah better. Can you make a list of some of the signs of Allah that you have seen in creation?

⚙ The orbit of the planets, the change from day to night, the movement of wind and rain, the changing seasons, the precision of sunrise and sunset, the bubbling of spring water, the growing of plants, the revival of trees in spring time...all of these natural phenomena are clear signs that Allah is managing not only our world, but the entire universe! You only need to look for such signs, and surely you will find them all around you.

⚙ Prophet Muhammad (s) once met a nomad and asked him, "How do you know Allah exists?" The nomad responded, "O Messenger of Allah, when I walk in the desert and see footprints in the sand, I know that someone has passed by here. Doesn't the vast sky, earth and all its creatures prove that a merciful God created all of this and guides it?" The animals and other wonderful creations are clear proof of our Creator!

Heavenly Trees

In a sermon the Prophet (s) once gave, he talked about Allah's rewards for people in the afterlife. The Noble Prophet (s) informed his companions, "Allah plants one tree in heaven for whoever says *SubhaanAllah* (glory be to Allah), one for whoever says *Alhamdulillah* (praise be to Allah), one for whoever says *La ilaaha illallaah* (there is no god except Allah), and another for whoever says *Allahu Akbar* (Allah is Great)!"

The Prophet's companions were delighted to hear this wonderful news and began doing some math to see how many trees they had earned in paradise over time.

One companion said: "O Prophet of Allah! We've said these blessed words over and over again! Paradise must be full of trees for us by now!"

The Prophet replied: "Surely you have cultivated hundreds and thousands of trees for yourselves, but beware! Your bad deeds will burn these trees away if you are not careful!"

Read to Succeed!

⚙ Many people cancel out their good deeds by performing bad ones! For example, it is a good deed to help someone in need, but if you keep reminding them that you helped them or selfishly expect them to do something in return, you will lose the reward as a result of your bad intentions! Performing a good deed is easy, but making sure you don't lose it due to a bad deed is far more difficult.

⚙ The blessings bestowed upon the dwellers of paradise will be a result of their own deeds. Just as we read in this anecdote, for every *dhikr* (remembrance) we say, Allah plants a tree for us in heaven. It is the same for the other blessings of paradise too!

⚙ Tradition tells us that reciting the phrases mentioned in this story cleanses us of our sins. One day, the Prophet (s) was walking with his friends when he reached a tree with dry, withering leaves. He shook the tree, causing the dry leaves to fall to the ground, and said: "The dhikr *'Subhaanallaahi walhamdullilaahi wa laa illaaha illallaahu waallaahu akbar'* sheds your sins just as these leaves fell from the tree."

⚙ Can you think of actions that might cancel out your good deeds? Think about what kinds of things you should avoid saying or doing to make sure your bad deeds don't outweigh your good deeds!

Biḥār al-Anwār, Vol. 93, P. 168

Value Your Blessings

Once, the Noble Prophet (s) spotted a bit of bread on the floor of his house. His wife was about to unknowingly step on it. It is disrespectful to step on food. Even worse, no one could eat the bread and it would have to be thrown away, becoming *israaf*, or wastage!

Prophet Muhammad (s) always told people to honor bread, and to never waste it or any other food. Before his wife could step on the piece of bread, he bent down and quickly picked it up. It was clean, so he put it in his mouth and ate it.

By doing so, he showed that bread should be respected and that wasting food, no matter how small it might be, should be avoided. He said to his wife, "Now that Allah's blessings are at our disposal, value them. If you lose them, they may not return easily."

We should always be careful with Allah's blessings!

Read to Succeed!

⚙ Bread is one of the most important blessings of Allah. The Ahlul Bayt (a) have spoken extensively about respecting bread! One day, Imam Al-Kadhim (a) was invited to someone's home for dinner. As dinner was being served, a big bowl of food was brought out with bread underneath. The bowl was placed on top of the bread instead of on the tablecloth. Imam al-Kadhim (a) took this opportunity to share the importance of bread with everyone: "We should respect bread! Let's not keep it under the bowl."

⚙ *Israaf,* wastage, is not limited to food. It applies to any and all of Allah's blessings. A man was once performing wudhu when the Noble Prophet (s) passed by him. The man was wasting water during the process. The Prophet (s) kindly reminded him, "We shouldn't waste water." The man asked, "O Prophet of Allah! Is there israaf even in matters like wudhu?" The Prophet (s) replied, "Of course, israaf is possible in all matters."

⚙ Try this: make a poster for your class or home encouraging people not to waste.

Biḥār al-Anwār, Vol. 66, P. 43

44

The Value of Each Creation

A man came to the Prophet (s) once, grumbling and cursing at the wind. He was angry that the weather was so windy. The wind kept causing his scarf to fall to the ground, and dust was constantly flying into his eyes!

The Prophet (s) advised him: "Brother, you should be more prepared for the weather. Do not curse the wind—it too is one of Allah's many workers and is just doing its job!"

The wind is one of Allah's many creations, just like humans and animals are. We have a purpose in this world, and other elements, like the sun, wind, or rain, do too! Even if that purpose is not obvious to us, we must trust that Allah created it for a reason.

Just as the sun, clouds, streams, and ponds are Allah's soldiers and workers, so too is the wind. Without gusts of wind, what would carry the clouds across the world to rain over farms and dry lands to provide them water? Getting angry at one of Allah's important creations is an ignorant and foolish thing to do!

After hearing the Prophet's (s) advice, the man agreed to avoid cursing like this in the future. The Prophet (s) explained to him, "Whoever curses something not worthy of being cursed can end up with the curse returning to *him*!"

All of creation serves a particular purpose in this world. If we are annoyed by something like the weather, we should pause and try to remember the ways it benefits our communities and our own lives every day.

Read to Succeed!

⚙ Those who inappropriately curse people, animals, or other creatures of Allah are only harming themselves. After all, our words do not disappear into thin air after being spoken. Based on the Prophet's (s) narration, an undeserved curse returns to its sender.

⚙ Once, a rooster crowed loudly. A nearby Muslim said, "May Allah curse this bird!" The Prophet (s) said, "Refrain yourself! What you say is wrong, this rooster is calling us to prayer."
Muslims must always be careful with their words! When you cannot think of a good thing to say, either keep quiet or do *dhikr* of Allah. Instead of cursing, give thanks to Allah by saying alhamdulillah, or ask for forgiveness by saying astaghfirullah.

Temporary Happiness

The Noble Prophet's (s) home was a simple one. Like all of the other houses in Medina, it was made of sun-dried bricks and clay. The Prophet (s) was simple and humble, and the way he lived was proof of it. Even the furniture in his house was ordinary. The floor was covered by a simple mat and there was nothing expensive or even decorative in the house. It looked no different from the poorest person's house.

One day, a neighbor visited the Prophet's (s) house. He looked around at the simple decor and said, "O Prophet of Allah! You are Allah's messenger and the best of His creation. Roman and Persian kings have gold thrones and soft, plush beds lined with jewels. They lead such comfortable lives! You are like a king to us, so why do you live so simply?"

Clearly, this man did not understand the difference between a prophet and a king. Kings are *worldly* leaders. They often become greedy and materialistic, and want every possible luxury and comfort for themselves. The Messengers of Allah, however, are meant to bring lasting comfort for their people! They know that life is simply a path to the hereafter. Unlike kings, prophets can never ignore the problems their people face. If people are hungry or sick, prophets make it their duty to help feed them or nurture them back to health. They know that Allah will reward them on the Day of Judgement.

"Worldly happiness and comforts are short-lived," the Prophet (s) answered. "Our true comfort awaits us in the hereafter!" The Prophet (s) was not attached to this life or any of its luxuries, and we should try our best to follow his example!

Read to Succeed!

○ The world is not permanent for human beings, so we should avoid getting attached to its pleasures. There is no harm in enjoying worldly pleasures, but we should avoid spending excessively and being selfish. In this world, our job is to do our best to be good people who can enter paradise. This means we should work hard and use what we have earned for our worldly happiness as well as helping others.

○ Here are some other narrations about this world being temporary:

The Prophet (s):
- "The world is a cultivating ground for the hereafter." That means the seeds we plant today, we hope to harvest in the next life.

Imam Ali (a):
- "The world is a path, not a destination."
- "The world will end but the hereafter will always remain."

Imam Ali an-Naqi (a):
- "The world is like a marketplace where one group profits and another suffers loss."

○ Our blessed Prophet (s) only had possessions that he absolutely needed. Can you find a few things around your house that you no longer need? If they are items someone else might need, can you find a way to give it to them?

Conversations with Allah

Once, the Noble Prophet (s) was sitting in the masjid when a man came in. Quickly, the man said "Allahu Akbar" and began his prayer. The Prophet (s) watched as the man quickly recited Suratul Hamd and a second Surah, then bent for ruku. He went into sajdah even *faster*! Barely a minute had passed, and the man was finished with his prayers!

Prayer is how we communicate with the All-Merciful Allah. It should be offered slowly, calmly, and with one's full attention. Verses of the Holy Quran that are recited during prayer should always be spoken carefully and with correct pronunciation. If you rush through prayer and jumble verses together, you could pronounce them wrong, and say something other than what they truly mean!

Think about prayer as a conversation with Allah. Why would you want to rush through something as wonderful as a chance to speak to your Creator? Prayer is a time to think deeply about all Allah has blessed you with, and to make du'a for what your heart desires.

Why, then, did this man offer his prayers so quickly? Didn't he want to have that conversation with Allah?

The people who were sitting there and watching were shocked. They asked the Prophet (s) what he thought about the man's quick salaah.

The Noble Prophet (s) replied to his companions, "This type of prostration is like the quick pecking of a crow. If he dies after praying like this, he will not leave the world as a true follower of my religion!"

Ḥikāyatnāmeh Payāmbar, Vol. 2, P. 318

The man did not benefit from the salaah and therefore the salaah did not help guide him to be the best of people.

The Prophet (s) was not trying to insult the man or point out his flaws. The man's actions gave the Prophet (s) an opportunity to teach his companions what *not* to do. Of course, the Prophet (s) then approached the man to talk to him about his prayers and how he could improve them.

When the Prophet (s) explained to him that prayer should be done slowly and calmly, the man was surprised. He did not realize what a big mistake he had been making by praying so quickly. Now he understood that prayer was his chance to communicate with Allah, and was excited for his next prayer. This time, he was going to pray *much* more carefully!

Read to Succeed!

- *Salaah* (prayer) has three major benefits:
  1. It brings us closer to Allah
  2. It cleanses our souls
  3. It encourages and recharges us to perform good deeds

- These benefits, however, are a result of praying *correctly*. Praying too quickly or at the last possible moment means we are thinking of prayer as a chore, and it will not have a beneficial impact on our souls!

- Once, a man praying behind the Noble Prophet (s) was cracking his fingers during his prayer. After they had finished praying, the Prophet (s) commented, "Know that this (playing with his fingers) was the sole benefit you have derived from your prayer!" When we are distracted or fiddling around, our prayers are less meaningful. Try your best to maintain focus in your salaah!

The Wise Young Man

A young man once visited the Noble Prophet (s) and happily greeted him. He was delighted just to be in the company of the Prophet (s), and could not stop smiling! The Prophet (s) asked him, "My friend, do you love me?"

The man replied, "Without a doubt, O Prophet of Allah (s)! Of course I love you!"

"Do you love me as much as you love your eyes?" the Prophet then asked.

"I love you even more!"

"Do you love me as much as you love your father?"

"I love you more than I love my father."

"Do you love me as much as you love your mother?"

"O Prophet of Allah! I love you even more than her."

The Prophet (s) asked him all of these questions for a reason. He knew this young man was pious and intelligent. In order to show his companions how wise this young man was, the Prophet (s) then asked him, "Do you love me as much as you love your Creator?"

The young man responded, "By Allah, by Allah, by Allah, O Prophet! I do not love anyone as much as I love Allah. I love you because of my love for Allah."

The Noble Prophet (s) was overjoyed to hear the young man's wise response. He knew well that Allah was above and beyond any human being, and because of that, He deserved to be loved more than anyone.

The Prophet (s) turned to his companions and said, "You should all try to become like this young man. Love Allah for all the blessings and goodness He has bestowed upon you, and love me because of your love and adoration for Him!"

Ḥikāyatnāmeh Payāmbar, Vol. 2, P. 318

Read to Succeed!

- Words of wisdom are valuable no matter who they come from! Age doesn't determine whether a person is wise or not.

- One day Allah said to Prophet Dawood (a), "Love Me, and do whatever will make people love Me." Prophet Dawood (a) said, "Dear Lord! I love You, but how can I make others love You?" Allah answered, "Remind them of My blessings, they will start loving Me."

Trust in Allah

While traveling during a war, the Noble Prophet (s) and his companions entered a valley and decided to rest there. Everyone put down their belongings to relax and get refreshed.

The Muslim army was spread all across the valley. Some people sat in the grass drinking water, and others lay under trees to rest their tired legs. The Prophet (s) chose to rest under the shade of a tree a little further off from the others.

Suddenly, it began to rain. Within an hour, the whole valley was flooded! The flowing water separated the Prophet (s) from his companions completely, and he could not reach them. The heavy rain even made it difficult for him to see. The Prophet (s) was stranded, and completely alone.

The enemies of Islam knew this would be a good opportunity to attack. They began to move into the valley, looking for Muslims to fight. One of the enemy soldiers saw that the Noble Prophet (s) was alone by a tree, and decided to go and kill him. He told his friends, "This is my chance! I am going to go and kill Muhammad!" He mounted his horse and rode toward the Prophet (s).

He reached the Prophet (s) in no time, and dismounted from his horse right in front of him. He arrogantly said, "O Muhammad! Who can save you from me now?"

The Prophet (s) was not even the slightest bit scared. As the man drew his sword and began walking toward him, the Prophet calmly answered, "The Lord of both you and I."

In that very moment, the enemy soldier twisted his foot, fell flat on his back, and his sword fell to the ground before he could hurt the Prophet (s)!

The Noble Prophet (s) quickly grabbed his sword and stood over the man. He asked, "Now tell me— who will save you from *me*?"

Biḥār al-Anwār, Vol. 2, P. 179 & 174

The soldier was terrified and said, "Your grace and mercy, O Muhammad!" By saying this, he was trying to appeal to the Prophet's mercy. Even non-Muslims knew that the Noble Prophet (s) was a kind man and often forgave sinners. The Noble Prophet (s) forgave him immediately and set him free.

The enemy soldier was so impressed by the akhlaq of the Noble Prophet (s) that he knew he had to be a true messenger of Allah (swt). He stood and said, "O Muhammad! By Allah, you are a better man than I am!"

Read to Succeed!

⚙ A true believer never loses hope in Allah's mercy. In this story, we see how the Prophet (s) maintains his faith in Allah even in the face of death!

⚙ There are various degrees of forgiveness, and the Prophet (s) was at the highest level. We can see how deep his capacity for forgiveness is, because he forgave someone who, only a few moments before, threatened to kill him! One day, a man was brought to the Noble Prophet (s). His companions told him, "O Prophet of Allah, this man wanted to kill you." The accused man was terrified. The Noble Prophet (s) kindly said to him: "Don't be scared! Even if you had such an intention, you haven't harmed me yet." He then forgave him without another thought! SubhaanAllah!

Superstitions

Allah blessed the Noble Prophet (s) with a son, who he named Ibrahim. Unfortunately, Ibrahim did not live for very long, and passed away as a child due to a serious illness. By coincidence, a solar eclipse happened on the same day as Ibrahim's death.

A solar eclipse is an astronomical occurrence when the moon passes in front of the sun and blocks the sun's light from reaching the earth. It happens naturally, and has nothing to do with anyone's death. However, some people at the time thought that the sun had been eclipsed because the Prophet's (s) son had died! This idea was illogical, and even more alarming, it was a foolish superstition.

When the Prophet (s) learned about the people's superstitious beliefs, he gathered them and said: "O people! The sun and the moon are two signs of Allah, the Great. They only obey the word of their Lord, and no one else! Neither the sun nor the moon are ever eclipsed because of the birth or death of a person."

The people listened closely and realized they were wrong to draw such incorrect conclusions. The Noble Prophet (s) did not like for his friends or townspeople to believe in superstitions like that, nor did he like for them to find irrational links between events.

Biḥār al-Anwār, Vol. 81, P. 380

Read to Succeed!

- Islam is a religion of knowledge and wisdom, and no Muslim should accept illogical ideas, or base their lives on them.

- After the Noble Prophet's son Ibrahim died, two other incidents took place, which reinforced two important lessons. Let's consider them:

  - When Ibrahim was being lowered into his grave, the Noble Prophet (s) started crying. His crying triggered the Muslims to cry and they all mourned in unison. A few, however, wondered why the Prophet (s), who always encouraged others to be patient, was now crying. The Noble Prophet (s) said to them, "The eye weeps and the heart aches, grief and sadness are natural, but what is important is that we should not say anything that will displease Allah even in these hard times."

  - Once Ibrahim was buried, the Prophet (s) noticed a crack in the mud walls of the grave. He filled the crack with his own hands, and leveled it. Once done, he explained: "Whenever anyone of you performs a task, it must be done correctly." Even though the Prophet was going through a difficult time, he still made sure he did his work properly!

Taming the Wild Camel

In one of the orchards of Medina, there lived a camel that had gone wild and often attacked anyone who came too close to him. No one dared to approach the camel out of fear that it would harm them, and the camel's presence made the orchard unsafe for anyone to visit.

The caretakers of the orchard decided to approach the Noble Prophet (s) and ask him for help. After they explained the situation, he accompanied them to the orchard to try and solve this problem. They all cautiously entered the orchard, terrified of how the camel would act, but the Prophet (s) entered bravely and began calling out to the camel.

Suddenly, the camel appeared from behind a tree. Everyone looked around apprehensively, fearing that the Prophet (s) would be attacked. However, the camel came calmly toward the Noble Prophet (s). It kneeled before him and placed its head on the ground, as if it was prostrating before the Prophet (s). The camel's actions showed everyone that it felt love for the Prophet (s) the same way people did. Clearly, this camel knew the Prophet (s) was a Messenger of Allah!

The Noble Prophet (s) gently placed a hand on the camel's side and guided him over to its owner. By this point, much to everyone's surprise, the camel had calmed down completely!

One of the companions asked, "Do animals also know that you are a Messenger of Allah?"

"Yes," the Prophet (s) replied. "All creatures, whether they are humans or animals, are aware of my Prophethood."

Another companion said, "This camel bowed down to honor you. Allow us to prostrate before you, too! We want to honor you the same way!"

The Noble Prophet (s) shook his head, and refused to let his companions do such a thing. "No, my friends! Just like anyone else, I too will die one day. You should only bow before Allah, who is immortal and cannot die!"

Everyone was amazed to see how much respect the Prophet (s) received, even from an animal as wild and independent as this camel. More importantly, this showed them that love and reverence for Allah solves all problems!

Kanz al-Ummāl, Vol. 9, P. 272

Read to Succeed!

- Even animals recognized the Noble Prophet's (s) importance and came to him for help. Once, a companion of the Noble Prophet (s) secretly took a chick from a bird's nest he saw in a tree. The bird came to the Prophet (s) and started to circle around his head showing her distress. The Prophet (s) immediately understood the bird's actions to be its way of complaining, so he asked his companions, "Which one of you has bothered this little bird?" The companion confessed to his mistake, and the Prophet (s) instructed him, "Have mercy on this bird, and return the little chick that you have taken!"

- Animals recognized and loved the Imams as well. One day, Imam al-Kadhim (a) was invited to a friend's house for dinner. The Imam sat on a bench as he waited for their meal. The host went into the kitchen, and when he returned, he saw the Imam smiling. He asked him why he was smiling, and in response, the Imam pointed to the pigeons near the bench. He explained, "This pigeon said to the other, 'You are my comfort, and my love. By Allah, I love you more than everyone, except the man sitting near us on that bench.'"

CHAPTER 3

Developing Good Character

Bothering Others

It had been a long journey. For many days, the Prophet's (s) companions had been traveling the dusty roads of Hijaz under the scorching heat of the Arabian sun. They were headed to battle against the disbelievers of Mecca. Whenever they were too tired to keep going, they would stop and rest before continuing their journey.

One particularly hot afternoon, after riding for many hours, they stopped near a large and spacious resting place. Eager to eat and relax for some time, the army quickly dismounted from their horses and camels. Some were so exhausted that they couldn't even walk to the resting place and collapsed along the way! They dropped their belongings all over the ground and quickly fell asleep.

The army's belongings were scattered in every direction. Some of their bags were in the middle of the path, so people had to step over and walk around them. The other travelers staying there became annoyed by this inconvenience. When the Prophet (s) saw the mess the Muslims had created, he became displeased with his followers. He turned to them and said, "The rewards of jihad will not reach anyone who blocks the way of another, or who makes it difficult for people to pass." So, being tired was no excuse for poor manners or rude behavior.

The soldiers immediately realized that it wasn't fair for the resting area to be littered with their belongings, especially when it made it difficult for others to move around easily. They promptly collected their belongings and moved them out of the way. Once that had been taken care of, they knew they could rest and regain their strength!

Sunan Abī Dāwūd, Vol. 1, P. 592

Read to Succeed!

- Allah has given us many opportunities to be rewarded for our good deeds. However, we must be cautious not to lose our rewards by behaving inappropriately. In some cases, a single bad deed can erase all of our rewards! We must always consider how our actions will impact others. Being insensitive to others, even unknowingly, is unfair to them. One example of insensitivity is bad breath. Once, while sitting in the masjid, the Prophet (s) was approached by a man who sat by him and asked him many questions. It was clear from the man's breath that he had just eaten garlic. The foul odor reached the Prophet (s) and the companions gathered around him. The Prophet (s) didn't want to hurt the man's feelings by singling him out, so he made a general comment, "Whoever eats garlic should be careful their breath does not bother others." The Prophet (s) has also said, "Whoever bothers a believer, it is as though he has bothered me; and whoever bothers me, it is as though he has bothered Allah."

- Rather than point out flaws and mistakes that other people make, you should focus on yourself - how can you improve *yourself*? How can you make sure you are the best person you can be?

- Imam Ja'far as-Sadiq (a) has said, "By Allah, the good doers are successful! Do you know who they are? They are those who do not hurt even a small ant." We can see from these examples that not caring for others can be as hurtful as intentionally hurting them, and as Muslims, we should always be sensitive to the needs of those around us.

The Champion of all Champions

A group of young boys were having a weightlifting competition. Each of them took turns lifting heavy rocks and stones to see who among them was the strongest. Whoever could hold the heaviest object above his head would be crowned the champion. It was an interesting event to watch, and young and old gathered around to see who would emerge as the champion.

Each young weightlifter raised a rock and held it above his head for others to see his strength. They sweated heavily, huffing and puffing, as they took turns lifting heavier rocks. Each boy seemed to be strong, but the question remained: who was the strongest?

Prophet Muhammad (s) was walking through the neighborhood and came across the young weightlifters and their competition. He came closer, greeted them and asked, "What are you boys doing?"

One of them answered, "Walaikum salaam, O Prophet of Allah, we are having a weightlifting competition to see which of us is the strongest!"

The Prophet (s) asked, "Would you like me to tell you who the strongest among you is?"

The boys looked at each other, surprised at this opportunity. They nodded excitedly at the Prophet, eager to hear his answer. Who could be a better judge of strength than the Noble Prophet (s) himself?!

The Prophet smiled and said to them, "The strongest one among you is the one who can control his emotions the most when he is angry."

There was complete silence as the boys absorbed the Prophet's (s) words. The competitors' eyes fell to the heavy rocks they lifted only moments ago. They thought about their daily interactions and how they often failed to control their anger. Swallowing their moments of anger was definitely much more difficult than lifting these heavy rocks! The young boys learned that true champions display inner strength, not outer, physical strength.

Read to Succeed!

⚙ There are two groups of champions, each possessing a different power: one consists of people who are strong physically, but weak in controlling their anger. The other group consists of those who have strong control over their anger, even if they are not the strongest physically. In this story, the Prophet (s) identified the characteristics of both types of champions to the youth of Medina.

⚙ There is in fact *another* group of champions: they have a strong body and a strong soul. Such people are considered the best of all the champions because they have acquired both types of strength! Imam Ali (a) is the best example of this kind of champion. He was strong and brave in defending Islam, but gentle and calm when dealing with people every day. He overpowered Amr bin Abdawud, the Champion of Arabia, in the Battle of the Trench, and also single-handedly lifted the gigantic fortress gate of Khayber in the battle of Khayber! However, Imam Ali (a) would never show anger when ignorant men insulted him. He used his physical strength only to serve Islam and mankind.

The Blessings of Prayers

There once was a young man who always prayed in congregation, and especially loved to pray behind the Noble Prophet (s).

This man was always careful not to miss congregational prayers. He also never grew tired of talking to Allah through prayer. He truly understood the beauty of *ibaadah,* or worship, and loved feeling like Allah purified his soul each time he prayed.

However, the young man also made mistakes, sometimes even sinful ones. People were surprised to see this and wondered how a person who was so dedicated to his prayers could ever sin. He was definitely not a bad person, and that made it even more surprising.

A group of men, puzzled by his contradictory actions, decided to ask the wise Prophet (s) about the matter. They went to him and asked, "O Prophet of Allah! We have seen a young man who always prays behind you, but then commits bad deeds later on! How can this be?"

The Prophet (s) explained to them, "One day, his prayers will prevent him from engaging in such bad deeds. If a believer prays with true faith and the intention to feel closer to Allah, surely their prayers will benefit them. If your intentions are good, they will guide you to the right path."

Prayers always affect the soul, but this happens when you pray with strong belief and focus. Eventually, the habit of praying will pull a person away from any bad or sinful deeds they might have taken part in before.

But, like all things, this process takes time. When you make it a habit to talk to Allah five times a day, eventually you won't be distracted by bad deeds anymore!

Eventually, the Prophet's (s) prediction came true. Over time, the young man began to transform, becoming a better person with each and every prayer. He asked for forgiveness for his sinful actions, and promised to do his best to avoid doing them again. With the blessings that his pure intentions in prayer brought to his life, he eventually found it easier to abandon bad deeds!

Read to Succeed!

⚙ In our lives we come across people who, at first, don't seem to be pious. However, over time, they transform into virtuous servants of Allah. This is why it is important that we never judge others — they could always repent and become even closer to Allah than us!

⚙ Some people ask, "Why pray? Allah doesn't need our prayers." Of course Allah doesn't need our prayers! *We* need them. Consistent prayers are what keep us from stepping off the right path.

⚙ Prayers also have the power to bring those who are lost back to the right path. There are countless examples throughout history where we can see how prayer transformed sinners into virtuous people.

Here are some sayings of our Noble Prophet (s) about prayer:

- "Prayers blacken the face of Shaytaan."
- "The five daily prayers are the light of the believer's heart."
- "Whoever takes prayers lightly is not from us."
- "Prayer is the key to all goodness."
- "Prayer is the key to heaven."
- "Prayer is the pillar of religion."
- "Prayer is the light of a believer."

Can you think of ways that prayers can help *you* improve?

The Importance of Hard Work

One of the Prophet's (s) companions became very poor over time. At one point, he did not have anything to eat, not even a morsel to feed his family. This poor companion tried and tried to find a solution for his poverty, but he couldn't! Helpless and struggling, he decided to visit the Noble Prophet (s) and ask him for help.

The companion explained his situation to the Prophet (s). The Prophet (s) did not have much money to offer the companion, but he *could* teach the companion skills to support himself in the future! To do this, the Prophet (s) said to him, "Bring whatever you have in your home to me!"

The poor man could not understand what the wise Prophet (s) was trying to do, but he still did as he was instructed. He returned quickly with the only two items he had in his house: a bowl and a placemat. The Noble Prophet took both items from the man and asked his other companions: "Who would like to buy this bowl and this mat?"

"I'll buy it for one dirham," came one answer. A dirham was too little an amount for the items, so the Prophet (s) called out again: "Who would like to buy them for a higher price?"

"I'll buy them for two dirhams," answered another companion. Since this was a more reasonable price, the Noble Prophet closed the deal and the poor companion now had two dirhams! The Prophet (s) instructed him, "Buy food for your family with one dirham, and a sickle[1] with the other."

The companion rushed to the market to buy both things. Once he delivered the food to his family, he hurried back to the Prophet (s) with the sickle he purchased. With one dirham, the man could only afford a broken sickle without a handle. The Noble Prophet (s) held up this broken tool and asked his companions: "Who can lend a handle for this sickle?"

---

1 An agricultural tool consisting of a curved metal blade with a short handle fitted on a tang.

"I can," came a reply. This man passed a handle to the Prophet (s), who kindly fixed the sickle with his own hands. He then turned to his needy companion and instructed, "Go and chop firewood with this. Collect whatever you find. Don't overlook any wood, not even wood you think is too small or useless!"

That evening, the poor man went to work with his sickle, collecting and chopping firewood. Just as the Prophet (s) had advised him to, he took every piece of wood he could get his hands on, whether it was big or small.

He worked hard for fifteen days and nights, sold the firewood, and slowly earned enough money to feed his family! By doing this, he was able to pull himself out of poverty. The man realized the favor the Noble Prophet (s) had bestowed upon him. The Prophet (s) taught him how to earn his own living!

Read to Succeed!

- The best help one can offer to those in need is to equip them with the tools and training to earn their livelihood. In this way, they can become independent and not need to rely on anyone else or resort to begging, which is exactly what the Prophet taught the poor companion to do.

- Whenever Prophet Isa's (a) companions grew hungry they said to him, "O Ruhullah! We are hungry." Prophet Isa (a) would hit his hand on the ground and miraculously produce two pieces of bread for each of them. Whenever they became thirsty, they said, "O Ruhullah! We are thirsty." The Prophet (a) would hit his hand on the ground and water would gush out to quench their thirst. They asked Prophet Isa (a), "Who could be better than us?! Whenever we get hungry, you provide us with food, and whenever we get thirsty you quench our thirst?" Prophet Isa (a) replied, "He who works and earns his livelihood is better than you." Upon hearing this, his companions started to earn their own living by doing the laundry of other people.

- Can you think of times when it is better to try and help yourself instead of asking others for help?

The Camel Race

In the time of the Prophet (s), people rode on horses, donkeys, and camels. The Noble Prophet's (s) camel was the fastest in the city, and always defeated other camels in races.

One day, a nomad approached the Prophet (s) riding a camel of his own. He was confident in the strength of his camel, so he challenged the Prophet (s) to a race. Clearly, the nomad wanted to prove to everyone that *his* camel was the fastest in the city. The Noble Prophet (s) accepted his challenge and within minutes, the race began!

As dust rose into the air behind them, both riders sped toward the finish line. The companions of the Noble Prophet (s) watched anxiously. They did not want the Prophet's (s) camel to lose. The nomad's camel was younger, so it was possible he could win the race.

As the dust settled, all could see that the race had come to an end. The nomad's camel was far ahead, which meant the camel of the Prophet (s) had been defeated for the very first time!

While the companions were sad to see the Prophet (s) defeated, he was not upset in the least! Sports are a fun source of entertainment, and we should not take them too seriously. They teach us how to win and lose without getting upset.

The Prophet of Allah (s) was a teacher, so he did not let this opportunity to teach his friends slip away. He said to his companions: "My camel had become very proud and arrogant, so through this defeat, Allah has humbled him."

They understood at last why the Prophet's camel had lost; for no one, not even a camel, should be arrogant. Sometimes, small moments of arrogance can build up and become a much bigger problem. That was the case here, as the camel was accustomed to winning every time!

With this defeat, the Prophet (s) showed his companions that there are lessons to be learned even from being defeated.

Read to Succeed!

- This anecdote shows that the Noble Prophet (s) used to exercise regularly and encouraged healthy entertainment. As Muslims, we should try to adopt his behavior and, in addition to our daily worship and supplications, get involved in exercise and other healthy forms of recreation.

- The Prophet (s) was a skilled teacher. He taught his companions that even if the best of the best become arrogant, their pride will catch up to them, and they will eventually be defeated.

- If one loses, he can always try to figure out the reason for his loss to and avoid similar outcomes in the future. In our own lives, we should all strive to be good sports and have a good attitude no matter the outcome!

Family is Allah's Mercy

There once was a young man who had not been on good terms with his aunt for quite some time. He loved his aunt, but because of a minor argument long ago, they had stopped talking to each other. Ever since that argument, he had not paid her a single visit!

One day, the Prophet (s) was at the masjid talking to his companions about the importance of family. As the young man joined the group, he heard the Prophet (s) say, "Whoever among you has broken ties with his own family should not sit next to me today."

No one knew who the Noble Prophet (s) was referring to, but the young man took these words to heart—z he himself had cut ties with his own aunt. The Prophet (s) knew that the man was not speaking to his aunt, and used this moment to gently remind him to do what was right. Prophet Muhammad (s) was so subtle that not a single person realized he was referring to the young man!

Ashamed, the young man knew he had to speak to his aunt right away. He was grateful the Prophet (s) did not say anything to him directly and spared him the embarrassment. The man quietly stood up from among the Prophet's (s) companions, and headed straight towards his aunt's home.

She was surprised and incredibly happy to see him. They both knew how much they loved each other, so they made up and vowed not to let small matters affect their family again. Now that the relationship had been properly mended, the young man was content and happily returned to the Prophet's (s) gathering.

As the young man approached the group once more, the Prophet (s) said, "If, in a group, any one person breaks ties with a family member, the whole group will be deprived of Allah's mercy."

Kanz al-Ummāl, Vol. 3, P. 765

Whoa! So *that's* why he couldn't stay among them! No one would ever want to be excluded from Allah's mercy. Clearly, we should make the effort to maintain good relations with our families. When we do the right thing, we also make sure that others do not lose Allah's mercy because of our mistakes.

The young man was relieved that this barrier to Allah's mercy was now gone. He sat back down and happily listened to the Prophet (s) as he spoke, grateful to be able to benefit once more from his wisdom!

Read to Succeed!

⚙ Some sins are so terrible that not only the sinner, but even those who sit in his company are deprived of Allah's mercy. Breaking ties with one's family is one such sin.
There are disagreements in all families, but they should not grow into hatred or bitterness. In Islam, arguments should not extend beyond three days. The more time passes, the harder it becomes to mend the relationship. Bad feelings for one another can easily grow stronger if the issues are not addressed soon. Did you notice that the Prophet (s) did not yell at the young man or embarrass him in front of the others? The Prophet (s) was showing us that we need to look at our *own* behavior and handle such affairs privately. He was also showing us how to politely tell someone about their mistake.

⚙ Maybe the young man was right and his aunt was wrong. Do you think he should still be the one to fix the problem? Yes! It doesn't matter who is at fault, family ties need to be repaired by facing our problems directly and gently. We all need forgiveness, and we all need to practice offering forgiveness.

⚙ Narrations by the Noble Prophet (s) regarding maintaining family ties:
1. Maintain ties, even if it is through a single salaam.
2. He who has broken off with his family cannot enter heaven.
3. Maintaining ties increases one's lifespan and drives away poverty.
5. Don't break ties with your relatives, even if they break ties with you.

Come On, Let's Wrestle!

Prophet Muhammad (s) once came across a shepherd who was taking his sheep to graze in a valley outside Medina. This shepherd was strong and muscular, and many people claimed he was practically invincible. The man arrogantly greeted the Prophet (s) and challenged him, "O Prophet, have a wrestling match with me! If you win, I will give you one of my sheep."

This shepherd was not Muslim, and was probably just curious to see how the Prophet (s) would respond to his request. Was he really as kind and decent as the Muslims claimed?

The Noble Prophet (s) considered this offer, then said, "I will not accept your sheep, but if I win, I would like to have a discussion with you about the truth of Islam!"

The shepherd thought about it and agreed, and with that, the wrestling match began!

The Prophet (s) and shepherd began to struggle with each other, and within moments the shepherd was defeated! The Noble Prophet (s) brought him to the ground with ease, quickly finishing the match before it really began!

The shepherd could not believe how quickly he had lost. Handling this defeat was difficult due to his pride. He wanted to regain his confidence, so he challenged the Noble Prophet (s) to one more match. He dusted off his clothes and asked the Prophet (s), "Would you like to wrestle me again?"

The second match began, and again, the shepherd was quickly defeated. As much as he tried, he could not beat the Prophet (s)! Though the Noble Prophet (s) had now defeated the shepherd twice, he

was careful not to utter a single word that might upset the shepherd. The Prophet (s) could have easily mocked or humiliated him, or began bragging about his skills. But out of kindness, he did nothing of the sort, and instead, offered a hand to help the shepherd up off the ground.

The shepherd stood up with his help, and was impressed by the kindness and maturity of the Noble Prophet (s). He was amazed the Prophet (s) was so humble, despite winning so many times! Most other men that the shepherd knew were far more arrogant. Curious about where this humility came from, he began asking the Prophet (s) about Islam. SubhaanAllah! The Prophet (s) was beginning to guide this man, all because of his behavior!

By treating the shepherd with kindness and humility, the Prophet (s) was showing him the values of Islam. Instead of trying to convince the shepherd that Islam was the true religion, the Prophet (s) showed him with his actions. His manners and good sportsmanship spoke more than any lecture possibly could!

Ḥikāyatnāmeh Payāmbar, Vol. 6, P. 168

Read to Succeed!

❀ Many disbelievers became Muslim because of the Noble Prophet's (s) incredible manners and behavior. When they witnessed his good morals, they couldn't help but like the Prophet (s). His great character caused them to think more carefully about his message.

❀ After speaking with him or interacting with him, people could see clearly that the Prophet (s) was not after power, money, or any worldly gain. It was clear that what mattered to him most was the wellbeing of everyone around him.

❀ The family of the Noble Prophet (s) similarly, guided many people through their good behavior. Once a Christian came to Imam al-Baqir (a) and making fun of his name said, "You are a *baqar!*" *Baqar* means 'cow' in Arabic. The Imam replied, "No, I am Baqir." The man then said, "You are the son of a black and foul-mouthed woman." The Imam replied, "If you are right, may God forgive her, and if you are lying, may God forgive you." The Christian was impressed with the Imam's simple, polite response, and it made him interested in Islam. Later, that Christian actually became a Muslim!

I'm Not a King!

A man approached the Noble Prophet (s) to discuss something. When he came close to him, he began to stutter. The man was intimidated! His hands and feet trembled, and he found himself unable to utter a single word. He probably thought that since the Noble Prophet (s) was so close to Allah, it would be difficult to talk to him. He kept sweating and gulping, but simply couldn't muster the courage to speak.

The Noble Prophet (s) could see that the man was nervous, and was too frightened to speak. To calm the man's nerves, the Prophet (s) decided to begin the conversation himself. The Prophet (s) said with kindness, "Relax, my friend! I am not a king that you should fear!"

These kind words made the man's fear disappear into thin air. He was surprised and relieved by the Prophet's friendly words. Suddenly, he felt at ease and started to speak.

Biḥār al-Anwār, Vol. 16, P. 229

Read to Succeed!

⚙ One of the great features of the Noble Prophet (s) was his humility. Not a trace of pride or arrogance could be found in him. Although he was the head of state, his behavior never demonstrated the power his position held. It is well known that whoever visited Medina could not recognize the Prophet (s) at first glance. His lifestyle, clothes, speech, and habits were just like other people's, so he was not easily distinguishable from normal citizens. He saw himself as a slave of God and often said, "Which slave is more of a slave of Allah than myself?"

⚙ Worldly kings and presidents usually like for people to fear them, whereas the Noble Prophet (s) did not want anyone to fear him. He used to say to people: "I, too, am human like you, with the exception of the revelation that comes to me from Allah."

Without A Mirror

One day, the Noble Prophet (s) was expecting a guest to come visit him in his home. Before receiving the man, the Prophet (s) wanted to make sure he was well groomed. At that time, there was no mirror in the Prophet's (s) house, so it was hard to comb his hair and check his appearance.

To solve this problem, he filled a bowl with water and placed it before him. He then used the reflection in the water as a mirror to groom himself.

As he set his hair, his wife looked at him, amazed. She knew how important it was to look neat and tidy, but she didn't know it was to be maintained even without a mirror. She said, "O Prophet of Allah! You are the best of all, you are the messenger of Allah! Since we don't have a mirror, why do you have to trouble yourself by looking into a bowl of water?"

Biḥār al-Anwār, Vol. 79, P. 207; Vol. 16, P. 249

The Prophet (s) responded, "Allah Almighty likes to see a believer groom and prepare himself before meeting his Muslim brother."

Moments later, the guest entered the room and the Prophet (s) welcomed him, well groomed at last!

Read to Succeed!

- The absence of a mirror is not an excuse for leaving one's self ungroomed. In this anecdote, the Noble Prophet (s) teaches us how even a bowl of water may be used to help us groom ourselves. If you could not find your comb one day, how would you make your hair?

- No matter how important a position we hold, we do not have the right to neglect grooming ourselves. Even though our Prophet (s) was the best human being ever and the greatest Messenger of Allah, he still considered it necessary to groom himself.

- A Muslim had grown his beard too long. On seeing him our Prophet (s) said, "How nice it would be if this man looked after his beard?" The man left and returned with a groomed beard. When the Noble Prophet (s) saw him, he said to his other friends, "Groom your beards like this man's."

Keeping a Promise

One day the Prophet (s) and a friend of his had plans to meet at a large boulder. Once there, his friend realized there was an errand he had forgotten to complete.

"You go and finish your task," the Prophet (s) told him. "I'll wait for you here."

His friend promised to return as soon as he could, then quickly left to finish his errand.

As time passed, the day grew hotter and hotter. It was getting harder to stand under the scorching heat of the sun. The heat was bothering the Prophet (s), but he continued to wait for his friend at the promised spot.

People walking by saw the Prophet (s) sweating under the sun, and advised him to move. "Why don't you rest under the shade, or in a house? This heat is intolerable, you can wait for your friend some place where it is cool!"

The Prophet (s) did not accept anyone's suggestions. "I promised my friend I would wait for him here, not somewhere else! If he honors his promise to return, I must honor my promise to wait."

Biḥār al-Anwār, Vol. 16, P. 239

The Prophet (s) was honest and disciplined in everything he did. If his friend returned and did not find him there, he would think that the Prophet (s) had broken his promise! So, the Prophet loyally stayed where he was and waited.

Finally, his friend returned. The Prophet (s) smiled, glad to see they had both honored their word. His friend was grateful to see the Prophet (s) still waiting for him, and surprised that he had kept his promise so firmly!

Read to Succeed!

- In this story, the Prophet (s) showed just how important it is to keep your word. When you make a commitment to someone, you are telling them that they can trust you. If you do not honor that commitment or break your promise, people may feel like you are not trustworthy or reliable. Even worse, you will lose their respect!

- Sometimes, it can be difficult to fulfill the promises we make. But that is not an excuse to let someone down. Just as our beloved Prophet (s) endured the heat in this story, we, too, should be willing to endure some inconveniences.

- The Prophet (s) said, "On the Day of Judgement, the closest to me will be the ones who are the most honest, loyal to their word, reliable, and friendly toward people."

Blessed Hands

After the Battle of Tabuk, the Muslims returned to Medina as victors. Those who had stayed back rushed forward to greet their war heroes. Sa'ad was one of the welcomers. As he greeted Prophet Muhammad (s), he extended his hand, and the Prophet (s) shook his hand.

The Prophet (s) noted a difference between Sa'ad's hand and the hands of others. Sa'ad's hands were rough and coarse, as though he often used them to do difficult, manual labor.

The Noble Prophet (s) asked him, "What has caused your hands to become so rough and cracked?"

"I have to work in the fields to earn a living," Sa'ad replied. "I am either working at the farm with a spade, or drawing buckets of water from the well to water plants and trees. My hands always hold either a spade or a rope. Such hard work has caused my hands to become as rough and cracked as they are!"

Prophet Muhammad (s) was pleased to hear Sa'ad's reply. He was proud to see intelligent and hardworking people. In order to encourage Sa'ad, he kissed his hand. He then lifted Sa'ad's hand into the air, and announced to everyone, "This is a hand that will never burn in hellfire!"

Read To Succeed!

⚙ Honest and hard work has great significance in Islam. There are many narrations from the Noble Prophet (s) regarding the value of hard work: He who strives to earn a living for his family is like one who struggles in the way of Allah. Anyone who makes the effort to earn a halal livelihood is forgiven for their sins.

⚙ Whoever earns and lives off his own earnings, Allah looks kindly and mercifully at him. One day, Imam al-Kadhim (a) was working on a farm, dripping with sweat, when a man approached him and said, "Where are your servants who should work for you instead?" The Imam responded, "He who was better than me and my father also worked on the land himself." "Who was he?" The man asked. "He was the Noble Prophet (s), and Ameerul Momineen (a), and all my grandfathers. They all worked with their own hands."

⚙ Imam as-Sadiq (a): Ameerul Momineen (a) used to dig and cultivate seedlings. He used his hard earned money to buy and free a thousand slaves.

Caring for the Ill

Once there was a man on the streets who was behaving very strangely. A crowd formed around him, and everyone was entertained by his strange movements, funny actions, and dirty, ripped clothes. People thought he was putting on a performance, and laughed at his every move. He looked like a mess, but everyone thought he was harmless and funny.

The crowd grew bigger with every passing minute, and the laughter and yelling grew louder and louder.

After some time, the Noble Prophet (s) passed by. He saw the huge crowd, but could not see the source of their amusement.

He asked the man closest to him, "Why have you all gathered here?"

"O Prophet (s) of Allah, we are laughing at this crazy man," the man explained. "His actions are so strange!"

The Prophet's (s) heart saddened as he caught a glimpse of the man everyone was laughing at. He saw the man's disheveled appearance, confused expression, and jerky movements, and understood that this man was mentally ill. He was behaving strangely due to a mental disorder, and no one seemed to realize it.

The Prophet (s) said, "This man isn't crazy, he is mentally ill. Crazy is the person who forgets their purpose, who walks the earth arrogantly, and doesn't spend their time preparing for the next world. The person you are laughing at is someone who needs help!"

The Prophet's (s) words had a profound effect on everyone, forcing them to think carefully about their cruel actions. Their laughter came to an end, and people began to leave in shame. The Prophet (s) and a few kind people stepped forward to lead the man to a safe place, and give him food and clean clothes.

Biḥār al-Anwār, Vol. 73, P. 233

Read to Succeed!

- There are several kinds of "madness". This story introduces one of them, called arrogance, or pride. Another is anger. Imam Ali (a) said, "Avoid anger for it starts with madness and ends with regret." He also said, "Anger is a kind of madness because an angry person becomes regretful later."

- Do you know why a proud person is considered "crazy" by the Noble Prophet (s)? Think about it: is it wise for a person who will die one day and turn into dust to feel proud? Is it wise for someone who is nothing compared to the grandeur of the universe to feel proud? How can one ignore his shortcomings and think that he is better and superior to others? Think, and you will find even more reasons why those who are proud are "crazy"!

Invitation Only

One day, the Noble Prophet (s) was visited by one of his companions, Abu Shuaib. Just one glance at the Prophet's (s) face made it clear to Abu Shuaib that the Prophet (s) had not eaten a proper meal in days. This was during a time when the enemies of Islam kept attacking Muslims, and food was scarce in the city. The war made it too dangerous for Muslims to keep working at their jobs.

Many Muslims had also been forced to leave Mecca and migrate to Medina due to the horrible oppression they faced from the enemies of Islam. For this very reason, the Muslims of Medina had to endure many hardships, and hunger was just one of the many problems they faced.

Despite being their leader, the Prophet (s) had been enduring pangs of hunger for several days, just like the rest of his Muslim brothers and sisters. His face had a pale sheen because he had gone so many days without a proper meal! Abu Shuaib was very disturbed to see the Prophet (s) suffering like this. He went to his housekeeper and told him to prepare some food for the Prophet (s) immediately. Abu Shuaib returned to the Prophet (s) and invited him and four other companions over to his place for lunch, which they all accepted gratefully.

When it was time for lunch, the Prophet (s) and his companions left for Abu Shuaib's house. On the way, they bumped into a Muslim brother and stopped to chat with him. When the man heard they were going to Abu Shuaib's for lunch, he asked the Prophet (s) if he could join them, despite not having been invited.

The men all looked at each other, unsure of what to do. The Prophet (s), however, knew exactly how to handle this kind of situation. He told the man that he could come with them, but needed Abu Shuaib's permission to join them for lunch. "I'm sure he would love to have you," the Prophet (s) explained, "but we will need to ask Abu Shuaib if it is alright. We have to make sure he has enough food for everyone!" Together, they all continued toward Abu Shuaib's house.

As they walked, the Prophet (s) explained the importance of being considerate to his companions. He, himself, never attended any meal without an invitation, nor did he take anyone with him without receiving permission to bring a guest. He knew he would have to speak to Abu Shuaib before taking the new companion inside because it was the considerate thing to do.

So, when he reached Abu Shuaib's house, he went inside alone to speak to him privately. "My friend, as we walked toward your house, another man joined us," the Prophet (s) explained. "Because this is your house, it is entirely your decision whether he can join us or not. Allah will surely reward you for inviting us to your home and providing all of us with a home-cooked meal."

The Noble Prophet (s) wanted to make sure Abu Shuaib knew that he was free to either invite the visitor in or politely refuse, in the event that he did not prepare extra food. Alhamdulillah, Abu Shuaib had prepared enough, so he happily welcomed the Prophet (s) and all of the companions into his home. They had a wonderful meal, and each left full and grateful for the company of such good friends.

Biḥār al-Anwār, Vol. 72, P. 285

Read to Succeed!

- Always make sure you are invited to an event before you decide to attend! If you show up at an event you were not invited to, you might embarrass the host or be a burden if they do not have enough food prepared for another person!

- If we are invited to a party, we should be careful to avoid inviting others along with us without checking with the host first. The Noble Prophet (s) said, "If anyone of you alone is invited for dinner, do not take your children along with you without getting permission, for it is inconsiderate to do so."

The Dangers of Being Dirty

Whenever a revelation was sent from Allah, Angel Jibraeel would always bring the message to the Prophet (s). Whenever that happened, the Prophet (s) would repeat the verse to his companions so they could hear Allah's message. The companions would listen with love and passion, memorize the verses immediately, and teach them to everyone they knew with great excitement.

One time, many weeks had gone by, and no new revelation had come. Some of the Prophet's (s) companions asked him, "O Prophet of Allah! Why is it that there has been no message for us recently?"

The Prophet (s) looked at them and said kindly, "Physical purity will lead to spiritual purity. Can everyone honestly say that they are in the best physical state to receive Allah's beautiful verses?"

The Muslims thought long and hard about what the Prophet (s) had said. Could it be that their lack of overall cleanliness had prevented them from receiving divine messages from Allah? The companions quickly went home to clip their nails and bathe. They wanted to be in the best physical state to please Allah, and were eager to receive His beautiful messages once more!

After they had cleaned themselves physically, they decided it would be even better if they were spiritually clean too! So, they did their best to let go of any jealousy or anger in their hearts by forgiving others and asking others for forgiveness as well.

Once people had begun to take care of themselves again, it wasn't long before Angel Jibraeel returned with a new verse for the Prophet (s) to deliver!

Biḥār al-Anwār, Vol. 76, P. 84

Read to Succeed!

⚙ A true Muslim is always careful with his hygiene and cleanliness. He showers regularly, brushes his teeth daily, and clips his nails every week. The Ahlul Bayt (a) always advised people to be clean. Imam ar-Ridha (a) said, "Cleanliness is from the morals of the Prophets!"

⚙ We use our hands often, and because of that, we should make sure they remain clean so we do not get sick. The more we use our hands, the more germs might settle under our nails and make us sick. The Noble Prophet (s) used to clip his nails every Friday before going for Jummah prayers. Cleanliness keeps us healthy, and our health should always be a priority!

Who is Better?

Once, the Prophet (s) entered the masjid and noticed that people had formed two different groups. One group was busy with different forms of worship: they prayed, prostrated, and recited verses from the Quran. The other group was busy studying different subjects, from math and science to Islamic principles and Quranic interpretation. Some people in this group were teachers, and others were students paying close attention.

The Prophet (s) observed both groups, and was happy to see his companions spending their time engaging in such productive activities. The Prophet (s) thought to himself, *Both groups are involved in good deeds. One group is busy with worship, while the other is occupied with learning and teaching. They are equal in value! Today, I will sit with those who are learning; after all, Allah, has sent me as a teacher for mankind.* He then sat down with the group that was teaching each other and joined right in.

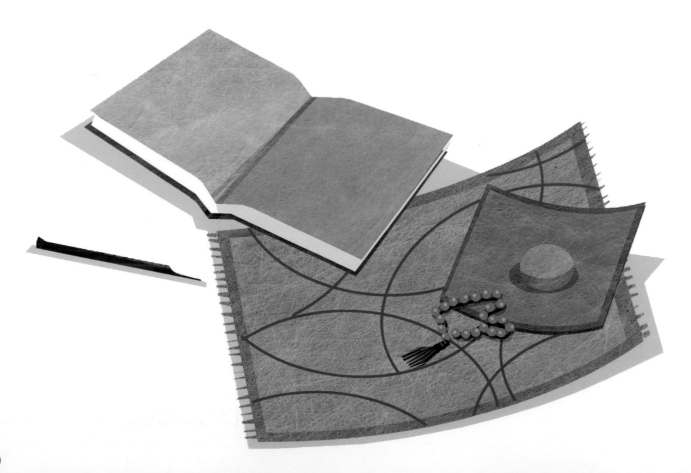

Read to Succeed!

- Here are some narrations regarding the value of knowledge and wisdom in Islam:

The Noble Prophet (s):

- The most valuable people are those who possess the most wisdom.
- Angels spread their wings under the feet of those who seek knowledge.

- Imam Ali (a):

- A seeker of knowledge will attain respect and good fortune in this world and the hereafter.
- No treasure is more valuable than knowledge.

- Imam al-Baqir (a):

- An hour of intellectual discussion is better than a night of worship.
- All earthly creatures, even fish in the oceans, send salutations and praise on the seekers of knowledge.

- We shouldn't limit the masjid to just a place for praying. As we see in this anecdote, learning and teaching sessions are also forms of worship that should also take place in masjids! What kind of programs does your masjid have?

- The fact that the Noble Prophet (s) introduced himself as a teacher sheds light on the holy nature of teaching. Teachers have the same work as prophets!

Al `Ilm Fil Kitāb Wassunnah, P. 312

90

A Promise Well Kept

Throughout his youth, Prophet Muhammad (s) worked as a shepherd. He would take his herd of sheep every morning to graze and bring them back at sunset.

One day, a companion said to him, "O Muhammad! I found a nice green field recently. Let's take our herds there tomorrow. What do you think?"

"Good idea," the Prophet (s) agreed.

The next morning, when the Prophet (s) reached the field, his friend had not arrived yet. The herd began pushing toward the field, but the Prophet (s) held them back. This was not an easy job, but the Prophet (s) and his friend had planned to visit this field together, and the Prophet (s) was not one to break a promise!

When his friend arrived, he noticed that the Prophet (s) was holding his herd from entering the grassland. He was surprised.

"Muhammad! You arrived first, so why didn't you let your sheep into the grassland?" he asked.

"Because we had decided to enter with our sheep together, and I didn't want to break my promise," the Prophet (s) replied.

When his friend heard this reply, he realized that Prophet Muhammad (s) was not an ordinary person. He was different from all his other friends, and more faithful to his word than anyone else.

The two smiled at each other, and proceeded to take their herds onto the field together, exactly as they had planned.

Read to Succeed!

- This anecdote shows that Prophet Muhammad (s) was a faithful and well-mannered person even before he announced he was a Prophet. Pastures are full of grass. No matter how many herds graze, there will always be plenty for other herds. If the Prophet's (s) sheep grazed on the grass sooner than those of his friend's, the second herd would not have remained hungry. However, the Noble Prophet (s) did not let his herd enter the pasture first, just to keep his word.

- You should keep the promises you make to people. If you break your word, people will have difficulty trusting you in the future!

CHAPTER 4

Treating Others Fairly & Justly

The Perfume Seller
Bilal's Adhan
Cheating Others
The Duel
The Slave Treated Like a Ship
Respecting Elders
The Humble, Hardworking Prophet
Camel or Sheep, It's All the Same!
A Piece of Hellfire
The Wrong Kind of Joke
The Rich, Arrogant Man
Even She Was Forgiven!
Teamwork

The Perfume Seller

Once, there was a perfume seller in Medina named Zainab. She would pack a basket with perfume each morning, and go door to door to sell them. Zainab had many customers throughout Medina, so she was able to earn a good amount of money as a perfume seller. People could always tell when Zainab had come by because the sweet smell of her perfumes stayed in every house she visited, even hours after she had left!

One day, Zainab headed toward the Prophet's (s) house. When she arrived, the Prophet (s) was not home. Regardless, the rest of his family welcomed her into their home and asked her to show them her new perfumes.

Zainab picked a variety of scents from her basket and showed them to the family. The room quickly filled with the sweet aroma of her perfumes, and the house smelled like a garden suddenly in bloom! The family spent some time trying samples of each wonderful scent and asking Zainab about their prices.

The Prophet (s) loved perfume and applied it often, so it was no surprise that his family enjoyed sweet scents, too! He always encouraged his family and companions to wear perfume and emphasized the importance of personal hygiene. Cleanliness and pleasant scents bring happiness and peace to our hearts, and remind us of heaven.

A few minutes later, the Prophet (s) returned home. It was obvious to him that Zainab was nearby from the sweet smells that lingered throughout the house. He entered and saw everyone gathered around her.

He greeted her happily with salam, and said, "Whenever you come, our home smells delightful! With the barakah and blessings of perfume, our entire house is full of goodness!"

Zainab was pleased with his praise and replied, "O Messenger of Allah, with your presence, you make these rooms much sweeter than any perfume!"

The Prophet (s) looked over Zainab's perfumes, and then gave her some advice. "Zainab, you have always been a good and honest person. Continue to be good and honest in your business. Do not be deceitful and don't cheat others; honesty is closer to piety and will always make your earnings blessed."

Biḥār al-Anwār, Vol. 22, P. 134

Zainab nodded in agreement, and silently promised herself she would always be honest in her business, just as the Prophet (s) had advised her. When everyone had selected their perfumes, Zainab packed her basket and left the Prophet's (s) house.

As she stepped out, she realized that she had earned something much more valuable than money from this trip. She learned an important lesson directly from the Noble Prophet (s) himself— a lesson about the value of being truthful and honest!

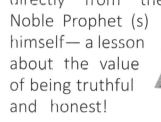

Read to Succeed!

- Some people think cheating and lying is the way to earn money quicker and in larger amounts. However, money that is earned unlawfully has no blessings and can never bring happiness or comfort to one's life. Instead, it only brings sadness and discomfort.

- On the other hand, lawful money is always blessed. If one is truthful and honest with customers, his or her business will flourish. It is for this very reason that the Prophet (s) advised Zainab not to cheat her customers. It is a sunnah of the Prophet (s) to apply perfume often, and Allah loves those who are clean and smell pleasant. We should apply perfume not just for other people, but to please Allah. By doing it for Allah, applying perfume can become an act of worship! Try and make it a habit to apply perfume or *itr* after a shower, after performing wudhu, or before leaving your house. Of course, don't forget the Islamic guidelines for applying perfume.

- The Imams (a) liked perfume, as well, and advised others to apply it. Imam ar-Ridha (a) said, "Applying perfume is among the manners of the Prophet (s)." Imam al-Kadhim (a) said, "A Muslim should apply perfume every day, and if he cannot do that, then every other day, and if he cannot manage that, then he should at least apply perfume every Friday."

Bilal's Adhan

The disbelievers of Mecca made life extremely difficult for the Prophet (s) and his followers, and constantly bullied and abused them. When the hardships became too unbearable, Allah ordered the Muslims to migrate to Medina, a city where they would be safe. Once there, the Prophet (s) established an Islamic government and took charge of the affairs of the Muslims who lived there. In a number of battles over time, the disbelievers of Mecca tried to crush the new Muslim community. However, they were never successful!

In the eighth year of Hijrah, after the disbelievers broke a peace treaty, the Prophet (s), under Allah's orders, decided it was time to free Mecca from its idol-worshipping practices. Thousands of Muslims marched towards Mecca and camped outside the city, completely surrounding it. The people of Mecca were terrified when they saw this and surrendered without a fight. Mecca was conquered without any bloodshed, and not a single life was lost.

It was then that the Noble Prophet (s) asked his companion Bilal to recite the Adhan (the call to prayers) from the roof of the Ka'bah. When the newer converts to Islam saw that a former black slave had been chosen for such an honorable task, they were shocked!

They expected the Prophet (s) to choose a prominent leader, or perhaps a wealthy community member for this honor, rather than a former slave. Bilal's previous status as a slave meant he was looked down upon by many other community members. As Bilal began to recite the adhan, the people began muttering amongst themselves. One man sneered,"It's a good thing my father isn't alive to see this day!"

"Looks like the Prophet could not find anyone better than a lowly slave for the task," another mocked.

Moments later, Angel Jibraael informed the Prophet (s) about the cruel remarks the people were making toward Bilal. Without a moment's hesitation, the Prophet (s) summoned these men. He reminded them that Islam teaches us to respect all people, regardless of their skin color, ethnicity, wealth, or social status. A white person is no better than a black person, and a leader is no better than a former slave. These worldly characteristics are not what make a person good in Islam. The Prophet (s) explained to them that true goodness is measured by *taqwa*, which is being constantly aware and conscious of Allah.

The men realized that their prejudiced and judgemental behavior was wrong, and immediately went to show Bilal their support and offer their friendship. Bilal was a good and pious man, and definitely the right man for the job!

Read to Succeed!

- By choosing Bilal as the Mu'adhin (the person who recites the call to prayer), the Prophet (s) established that the color of a person's skin should never be a basis for judgement in Islam. The color of your skin is how Allah has designed you, and everyone is Allah's precious creation. It is the character of a person and their taqwa that is truly important.

- Bilal could not pronounce the letter "sheen". This meant when he recited the Adhan, instead of "Ash-hadu" he would say "As-hadu". Despite complaints from some Muslims and their insistence on his removal, they could not convince the Prophet (s) to change his mind. He showed them that the sincere Adhan of Bilal was far better than an Adhan recited with the intention of showing off.

- Once an argument broke out between Abdur Rahman bin Awf, a wealthy and famous man, and one of his slaves. During the argument, he lost his temper and insulted his slave by making a reference to his race. When the news of this incident reached the Prophet (s), he immediately reminded Abdur Rahman about speaking to others respectfully and kindly, no matter who they are.

Cheating Others

One day, the Prophet (s) was walking through a busy street full of markets. There was a lot of hustle and bustle as people went about buying and selling their goods. In every corner, different types of products and produce were on display. One shopkeeper sold meat, while another offered colorful fabric. There was one who had fresh fruit spread out on a mat, and another who arranged his merchandise in a fancy pattern to attract customers.

As the Prophet (s) was strolling through, he noticed a man selling wheat. The yellow wheat lay gleaming in a pile on a mat. The Prophet (s) went towards him and noticed the excellent quality of the wheat at the top of the pile. The Prophet (s) commented, "You have such good wheat! How much does it cost?"

The man gave him a fair price. Before paying, the Prophet (s) placed a hand under the pile to check if the grain underneath was also of good quality. The wheat felt moist to the touch, and when the Prophet (s) removed his hand, he saw that it was rotting! The wheat seller had placed the good wheat on top in hopes that no one would notice the rotting wheat! The Prophet (s) was disappointed at the wheat vendor's actions and told him, "A person who tricks other Muslims is not a real Muslim."

Mīzān al- Ḥikmah, Ḥadith 14955 & 14956

Read to Succeed!

- Being a Muslim isn't just about having a Muslim name or being born into a Muslim family. Being a Muslim means to act and live as a Muslim should! One of the important qualities of a true Muslim is honesty.

- Honesty in business is very important. It is okay for a vendor to sell damaged goods as long as he or she does not hide its flaws from customers. The Prophet said, "A Muslim is not allowed to sell defective products unless he makes the defects known to the buyer." In another hadith, the Prophet said, "If one sells flawed merchandise as regular merchandise, he will cause the wrath of Allah to descend upon him and angels will curse him."

- A deceitful business man actually harms himself more than his buyers. He will lose the trust of his customers, and his income will never receive Allah's blessing! In fact, his earnings will be considered *haram and unlawful*. The Prophet also said, "Allah will remove happiness and blessings from the income of one who tricks his fellow brothers in trade."

The Duel

Once, two rams with large horns were dueling each other in an empty field. They collided head to head, pushing each other back, over and over. It was a match to be witnessed!

The Noble Prophet (s) and his companions watched as the match went on, and noticed that one of the rams was being much more aggressive than the other. The weaker, smaller ram looked tired and unhappy, as though he did not want to fight at all, but was only fighting in self defense.

Finally, the larger, more aggressive ram gave the smaller one a large blow, strong enough to push him to the ground and scare him. The injured animal quickly stood back up and ran away as fast as he could.

It was clear to everyone that this match was not a fair one. One of the rams had the advantage of being larger and stronger, and he used that advantage to bully the smaller, weaker ram.

The Prophet (s) used the rams as a metaphor to teach a valuable lesson. After watching the smaller ram run away, the Noble Prophet (s) said wisely: "By Allah, on the Day of Judgement, those who bully others will answer to Him for their actions."

Allah is the Most Merciful and Most Just! Through this story, the noble Prophet (s) is trying to teach us to treat others kindly and fairly, and that everyone, even animals, will have to pay the consequences for their actions.

Read to Succeed!

- The Noble Prophet (s) took every opportunity to remind everyone about the Day of Judgement. This story is an example of when the Prophet (s) gave one such reminder.

- If Allah will not ignore the oppression of one ram over another, then of course He sees the oppression of tyrants and dictators as well. We must not forget that Allah is All-Seeing, and justice will always be delivered!

- How do you think Allah feels about bullies? Here are some of the many narrations we have about oppression:
  - The Prophet (s) said, "Do not oppress, for it will darken your hereafter."
  - The Prophet (s) said, "Oppression leads to regret."
  - Imam Ali (a) said, "Do not oppress, for it is the greatest sin."
  - Imam Ali (a) said, "If you oppress, the very same oppression will destroy you."

- Imam al-Baqir (a) said, "My father embraced me on his deathbed and said, 'O son, I will give you the same advice which my father gave me. Son, do not oppress one who has no one to help him except Allah."

The Slave Treated Like a Ship

Once, there was a group of men who had set out for a long journey. After traveling for many hours without stopping, they became very tired and no longer had the energy to carry their luggage. They stopped to rest every now and then, but eventually, even these little breaks weren't enough— they were just too tired!

Sometimes, when we are tired, even light items feel like they are ten times heavier. When you are tired at the end of the school day, doesn't your backpack feel much heavier than it did when you left your house in the morning? These travelers felt the same way!

As they were passing through Medina, the travelers decided to take another short break. There was one slave among these travelers, and one by one, they all began to dump their belongings on him. Soon, he was loaded with a large amount of heavy baskets and bags.

From a distance, he looked more like a mountain of luggage than a human being! With his hands full of so many items, it was hard for him to walk, and impossible for him to rest like the others.

The Prophet (s) lived in Medina at the time, and happened to be passing by this group of travelers while they rested. He saw the slave struggling under the weight of so much luggage, and kindly patted him on his back.

The Prophet (s) warmly joked, "There is so much weight on your shoulders! With all of this cargo, you could be a ship!" The Prophet (s) smiled at the slave and began to help him remove all the luggage from his back. The slave was relieved that someone saw his suffering and stopped to help. For a moment, he forgot all about his burdens. Slaves were often mistreated by others, so it made him very happy to be treated with kindness for once.

Biḥār al-Anwār, Vol. 16, P. 294

The Prophet (s) knew slavery was a harmful practice, so he spoke to the travelers to free the slave. No man should be treated less than anyone else! That kind of cruelty goes against the teachings of Islam. The slave was overjoyed to finally be free, and thanked the Prophet for his kindness and fairness. As a free man, he did not feel as tired as he did before!

Read to Succeed!

- The moral of this story is that all people should be treated fairly, no matter what their status is. No one has the right to abuse or use any other person. The Noble Prophet (s) was the model of justice, and here he taught by example by not looking down upon the slave or neglecting him.

- Sometimes, a story can have symbolic value as well. The travelers were on a trip, and when they grew tired, they burdened the lowest-ranked person among them. Just like these travelers, each of us are on a journey as well — a journey through this life and all of its tests! There may not be slavery anymore, but think about the other small ways you might mistreat another person to lessen your burden.

- This anecdote shows the softheartedness of the Prophet (s). He was softhearted even towards his enemies. In the Battle of Uhud, several companions of the Prophet (s) were martyred, and he was severely injured. His companions said, "O Prophet of Allah! If only you had cursed these infidels, Allah would have destroyed them." He answered, "I have not been appointed as a Prophet (s) to curse people, but to guide them to the right path, and be a source of mercy for them." Then he prayed for the guidance of the very same infidels saying, "O Allah, guide this nation for they do not know."

- The Prophet (s) often made lighthearted jokes like the one in this story. Appropriate and kind jokes that do not hurt anyone's feelings have many benefits. They bring smiles to people's faces and bring them out of sadness!

The Humble, Hardworking Prophet

The disbelievers who opposed Islam always wanted to attack Medina, so the Muslims had to be careful and prepare for this possibility. If the disbelievers successfully entered Medina, it would be very difficult to fight them. The Muslims knew they had to prevent an attack at all costs to keep their city safe!

Everyone in Medina tried to come up with solutions, but no one could think of a foolproof plan to keep the disbelievers out. Finally, the Prophet's companion Salman had an idea.

"We could dig a deep trench all around the city," he suggested. "A trench will keep the enemy from advancing!"

A trench is a large and deep ditch. Digging one around the entire city of Medina would be a huge task, and everyone would have to help! There were no bulldozers or fancy tools at the time, so this job had to be done by hand.

Everyone approved of Salman's clever idea and agreed to the task. The entire community spread out to every corner of the city and rushed to start digging the trench. The Prophet (s) himself worked alongside all the other men. Just like every other member of the community, the Prophet (s) put in every effort to defend Medina.

The Prophet (s) was certainly the leader of the Muslims, but he did not use his status to avoid having to work. He considered himself to be equal to his fellow working Muslims. How many presidents or leaders can you think of who are willing to work with ordinary citizens? Very few, if any! It is the humble nature of our blessed Prophet (s) that makes him unlike any other leader!

At this time, the people of Medina suffered from a severe shortage of food. Many Muslims went hungry for days on end, and the Noble Prophet (s) was among them.

One day, Sayyidah Fatimah (a) took what little flour she had and baked bread for her sons, Hasan (a) and Husain (a). She broke a piece off and went to give it to her father, the Prophet (s). She knew how hungry he must have been, since he was working so hard in the scorching heat to dig the trench!

Biḥār al-Anwār, Vol. 20, P. 245

The Noble Prophet (s) was hard at work when she arrived to give him the small piece of bread. When he saw it in her hands, he asked her, "Where did you bring this bread from?"

Fatimah (a) replied, "I baked bread for my sons and brought a piece from the loaf for you!" The Prophet (s) told her, "This is the first morsel I have eaten in three days." Sayyidah Fatimah's (a) heart ached for her father, and she was glad to have brought him some food at last, and ease his hunger.

Read to Succeed!

- The Prophet (s) always consulted others, even in the most important decisions. He allowed everyone to give their opinion. In this anecdote, we see how he listened to Salman and accepted his suggestion to dig the trench.

- One of the titles of Sayyidah Fatimah (a) is 'Umm-e-Abiha' (the mother of her father) because she loved and cared for the Prophet (s) just like a mother would. This anecdote is just one example of her love for her father.

- Sayyidah Fatimah (a) was by her father's side in the hardest times of his life. One day, one of the disbelievers saw the Prophet (s) in the street and threw garbage on him. The Prophet (s) did not react and quietly returned home. When Sayyidah Fatimah (a), who was just a little girl at the time, saw her father, she cried bitterly and cleaned his head and face. He said, "Don't cry, my daughter! Allah will protect your father from the mischief of the enemies and will grant him victory over them."

Camel or Sheep, It's All the Same!

Many of the Noble Prophet's (s) companions in the region of Hijaz were shepherds and herders. The shepherds worked with sheep, and the herders worked with camels. The camel herders at the time were richer than the shepherds because everyone wanted to purchase a camel. Hijaz was a hot, dry area and camels were the perfect animals to travel with through the desert. They can walk for many miles without needing even a sip of water. Like cows and goats, camels also produce milk, which was the perfect, cool drink for a hot day. For all these reasons, camels in Hijaz were far more expensive than other animals, which meant that camel herders made more money.

Because of their success, camel herders thought their work was superior to the work of shepherds. Eventually, they began to think that they themselves were better than shepherds!

One day, a group of shepherds was sitting near a group of herders. The camel herders proudly said to them, "Our work is better than yours! We earn more money, and camels are bigger and more useful than sheep. How does it feel to be so much poorer than us?"

The shepherds were upset to hear this and tried to defend themselves and their work. No matter what they said, the camel herders kept loudly repeating that they were better than them!

When the Prophet (s) saw this happening, he knew he had to put an end to their bickering. The herders and shepherds both did important work and had no right to mock the other. It did not matter who made more money— what mattered most was that they were all reliable and hardworking men!

The Prophet (s) addressed both groups with an important reminder: "Prophet Musa (a) was a shepherd when Allah made him a Prophet, and so was Prophet Dawood (a). I myself used to work with sheep when I was appointed Prophet."

Even Allah's prophets were shepherds! How could any herder claim to be better than a shepherd after hearing this?

The shepherds were overjoyed to hear the Prophet (s) come to their defense. The camel herders realized their bragging was unfair to the shepherds. They apologized and promised to avoid that kind of arrogant behavior in the future.

After all, how could anyone look down on a job our Prophet (s) himself performed?

TRead to Succeed!

- No Muslim has the right to make fun of or humiliate another person. The Quran says, "O you who believe, do not make fun of others!" Bragging and boasting are bad manners. We should always try to invite people to Islam by treating them with respect and exercising our best manners.

- Making fun of others can take many forms, all of which you should avoid. Here are some examples we should never engage in:
  1. Making fun of how someone speaks or their accent.
  2. Making fun of someone's clothes, car, or house.
  3. Joking about someone's appearance or complexion.

- What mattered to the Prophet (s) was not a person's job, but that they worked hard at it! He once came across a man and asked his companions, "Does this man work?" "No," they replied. The Prophet (s) responded, "Then he has lost worth in my eyes."

- The Prophet (s) himself was a hard working man. He worked to earn his living, and did whatever job was necessary to help Islam. When the Muslims were building a masjid, he helped make the bricks and carry them. When the Muslims in Medina were being attacked, he helped dig the ditch to defend the city. Even when the work was difficult or dirty, and our Prophet (s) was well into his sixties, he continued to work his hardest. He always taught by example!

A Piece of Hellfire

Once, two men were arguing over a sum of money and both claimed it was theirs. When they could not agree on who it belonged to, they decided to approach Prophet Muhammad (s) and ask for his help.

Both men explained their side of the story in front of the Prophet (s) and requested that he act as a judge to end their dispute. The Prophet (s) listened to what they had to say and used the evidence presented to pass judgement, even though he had knowledge of the unseen.

Before judging between them, the Prophet (s) said, "If I award one person's money to another, the recipient should know that I have given him a piece of Hellfire."

The Prophet's (s) words caused the two men to think deeply. Through this warning, the Prophet (s) taught them that wrongfully claiming someone's property is a grave sin. It does not matter whether they forcefully take others' property or get a hold of it through trickery. They should not consider themselves clever because really, they are only collecting Hellfire!

The Prophet's (s) advice had such a profound effect on the two Muslims that they said to him, "O Prophet of Allah! We fear Hellfire and do not want to fight over this money any longer."

The Noble Prophet (s) encouraged them to settle the matter peacefully and amicably. The two then settled the issue and returned home.

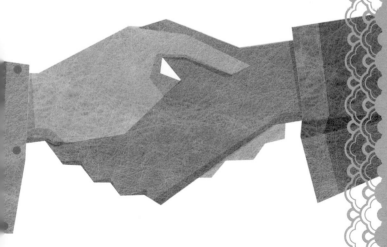

- The Prophet (s) has knowledge of the unseen and could have easily figured out who the money truly belonged to. Instead, he listened to the men tell their sides of the story and passed judgement based on the evidence and proof presented to him. The Prophet (s) wanted to show how to pass judgement according to the system as an example for us to follow.

- Remembering the Day of Resurrection keeps us from oppressing others, in addition to preventing us from committing other wrongdoings. If anyone truly believes and understands that on the Day of Resurrection all of our actions will be accounted for, they would never take someone else's property through fraud or disrespect others. This anecdote is a representation of how brilliantly the Noble Prophet (s) resolved the dispute by simply reminding them of the Day of Judgement.

- The punishment in Hell is a result of our own misdoings. Lies, theft, unlawful earning, usury and all such vices are pieces of Hellfire that people accumulate for themselves!

The Wrong Kind of Joke

Once, the Prophet's (s) companions were sitting together and chatting about their day. They were all tired after a long day of work, and were now trying to relax. To get comfortable, they all removed their shoes.

When one man turned away, another took his shoes and hid them under his clothes. He did this as a playful prank to see what his friend would say and do when he couldn't find his shoes!

A few minutes later, the owner of the shoes stood up to leave. He looked around for his shoes, but he couldn't find them. He was in a hurry and needed to leave immediately! He grew anxious and upset. He asked his friends, "Has anyone seen my shoes?"

The man who had taken his shoes laughed and said, "Here, I took them." He laughed again as he handed his friend the shoes, clearly enjoying the joke despite the unhappy look on his friend's face. The owner of the shoes took them without a saying word, put them on, and left in a rush.

The Noble Prophet (s) saw what had happened, and was displeased with the nature of this joke. The Noble Prophet (s) liked to joke around and be playful, but he knew that some jokes were unacceptable— particularly, jokes that hurt others or cause them stress or fear. Such jokes are at the expense of someone else, and are no laughing matter!

The Noble Prophet (s) turned to the man who played the prank. "Why did you worry and stress a believer like that?" he asked.

The man replied, "O Prophet of Allah! I swear I was only joking."

"That was not a joke," the Prophet (s) said. "A joke shouldn't cause fear or stress."

Ḥikāyatnāmeh Payāmbar, Vol. 8, P. 486

Read to Succeed!

🔹 Some people end up hurting others while thinking they are joking. Joking is meant to increase friendship and love, not hurt others. In this story we see how the companion's joke was an example of a bad joke.

🔹 Some people joke using foul language or name calling. Such humour often leads to animosity. Imam al-Baqir (a) said, "Allah likes people who lighten the mood with jokes, as long as they don't use abusive language."

🔹 There's a limit to everything, even joking. It is true that the Ahlul Bayt (a) have said, "a believer jokes," but excessive joking is not desired. Joking is like salt; it adds pleasure but should not be in excess.

The Rich, Arrogant Man

The Prophet (s) was friendly and warm and always willing to care for anyone who needed his help. A number of the Noble Prophet's (s) companions were poor, but that made no difference to him. Whether his friends were rich or poor, he loved them all equally. He would visit his less wealthy companions often and was like an older brother to many of them.

However, his friendliness toward the poor upset the wealthier people in town. They did not like seeing how easily the poor received the Noble Prophet's (s) help!

Once, one of the Prophet's (s) poorer companions came to visit him while a richer companion sat by his side. The rich man made a disgusted face, and pulled his robe away from the poor man because he was wearing expensive clothes.

The Noble Prophet (s) was saddened by the rich man's behavior, as he had told his followers several times that all Muslims were brothers and that no one should be treated differently based on their financial status.

The Prophet (s) asked the rich man, "Why did you do that? Are you afraid you will suddenly become poor by being near him, or that he will steal your wealth?"

The Prophet's (s) comment made the rich man bow his head in shame. He felt terrible for having been so arrogant, and wanted to compensate for his behavior. He said, "O Prophet of Allah! To make up for my mistake, I would like to give half of my wealth to this Muslim brother."

The Prophet (s) turned to the poor man and asked, "Will you accept half of his wealth?"

The poor man refused. When the Noble Prophet (s) asked why, he replied that he did not want to become arrogant like the rich man.

The poor man did not accept the rich man's offer. He did not want wealth to make him arrogant, for he knew how the pride of the rich hurts the poor.

Read to Succeed!

- The Noble Prophet (s) said, "On the Day of Judgement, God will disgrace he who humiliates a believing man or woman because of their poverty."

- We must treat all believers equally regardless of their social standing. Imam ar-Ridha (a) said, "Whoever greets a poor Muslim brother differently than a rich Muslim brother will confront the wrath of Allah on the Day of Judgement."

- The Noble Prophet (s) not only sat next to the poor, but he also spoke with them, heard them out, and solved their problems. Some wanted the Prophet (s) to distance himself from the poor and gather the wealthy around him. It was in response to such attitudes that verse 52 of Surah An'am was revealed and Allah asked the Noble Prophet (s) to never push away the believing poor.

Even She Was Forgiven

The Noble Prophet (s) had numerous enemies throughout his life. The idol worshippers of Mecca were one such group that considered the Prophet (s) to be an enemy. They forced people to worship idols and they hated the Prophet (s) because he was not an idol worshipper like them.

The second group who hated the Prophet (s) were those who oppressed the poor and profited of off them. The Noble Prophet (s) was against oppression in all forms and always fought against the oppressive elite classes. It was for this very reason that they didn't like him either.

The third group that disliked the Prophet (s) was a certain group of Jews. Although some Jews lived in Mecca peacefully with the Prophet, another group of them didn't want to live under the laws set by him. They did not believe that he was a Messenger of Allah, and although the Prophet (s) did not force them to accept Islam, they were angry at him for challenging their religion.

All three of these groups opposed the Noble Prophet (s), and some people among them even tried to kill the Prophet! However, none of these attempts were ever successful.

One day, a Jewish woman tried to kill the Prophet (s) by poisoning his food. Before she could do so, she was caught in the act and brought before the Prophet (s).

When the Prophet (s) asked her why she had tried to poison him, she replied, "I thought to myself, if you are just a worldly leader, then I will have relieved the people by killing you!"

Ashamed after seeing that the poison did not reach the Prophet (s), she realized her mistake and asked for forgiveness. She accepted him as the Prophet of Allah, and became Muslim.

When the Prophet (s) heard her answer, he forgave her. The Prophet was always merciful to people when they realized their mistakes!

Biḥār al-Anwār, Vol. 16, P. 265

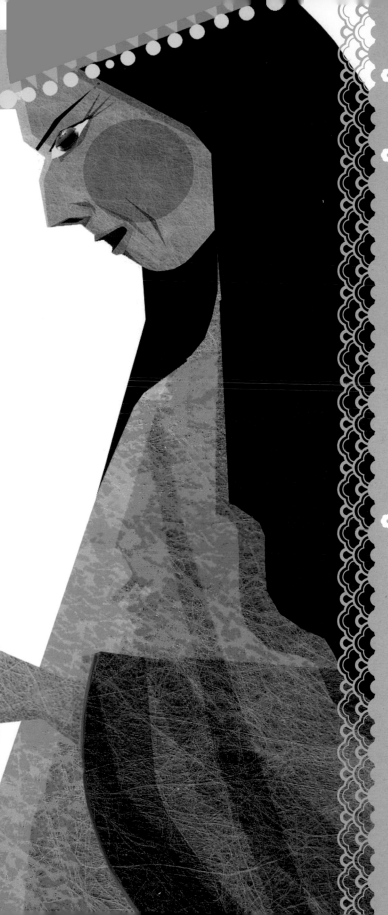

Read to Succeed!

⚙ The Noble Prophet (s) said:
Whoever forgives others, Allah, will forgive him.

⚙ Allah is forgiving and likes forgiveness too. The more one forgives, the longer he lives.
Imam Ali (a) said:

- If you overcome your enemy, thank Allah for this blessing by forgiving him.
- Forgiveness is the crown of good deeds.
- Forgiveness is the zakat of power.
- Forgiveness leads to respect and greatness.

Imam Husain (a) said:

- The most forgiving of men is one who forgives the very moment he has the power of revenge.

Imam as-Sadiq (a) said:

- Forgive, even the one who has oppressed you.

⚙ In the 8th year of Hijrah, Muslim soldiers marched to Mecca in order to free it from the infidels. On seeing the huge Muslim army, the infidels decided to surrender without fighting. Earlier, when the tables were turned, it was the army of non-believers from Mecca who gave the Muslims a hard time. After the conquest of Mecca, rather than taking revenge, the Noble Prophet (s) forgave the very Meccans who had previously been his enemies.

Teamwork

Once, the Prophet (s) and his friends were on a long journey. Every few hours, they would stop and rest for a while before continuing on their path.

At one of their stopovers they decided to slaughter a sheep to cook. They were all tired, so in order to do this, they had to divide the tasks and work together as a team.

One of the companions volunteered to slaughter the sheep, another offered to skin it, and a third one said he would do the cooking.

Another person was needed to collect firewood for the cooking, so the Prophet (s) happily volunteered for this task.

The companions said, "O Prophet of Allah! Please rest, and let us have the honor of cooking for you!"

The Noble Prophet (s) shook his head and replied, "I know you are great companions who want to serve and make Allah happy, but Allah does not like for anyone to consider himself above and beyond his friends. That includes me!"

Having said that, the Prophet (s) left to collect firewood, eager to put in as much work as his friends.

Read to Succeed!

- The Prophet (s) did not like arrogance or superiority in people. He never did anything to suggest he should be treated better than anyone else. Once, while he was circling the Ka'bah, his sandal broke. A man near him immediately took off his own sandals and offered them to the Prophet (s). The Prophet (s) declined his offer and said, "Thank you so much, but I don't like preferring myself over others."

- When working as a group, all members should pitch in to do the work so that the burden doesn't fall on any one person alone. Once, a group of the Prophet's (s) companions went for Hajj. On their return, they visited the Prophet (s) and praised one of their companions. They said, "O Prophet, whenever we stopped during our journey, he would recite, 'There is no god but Allah,' the entire time we were resting. He also did dhikr throughout the journey until the next time we stopped." The Prophet (s) inquired, "While he did this, who fed him and his horse?" "We did, O Prophet," they replied. "Then you are all better than him," the Prophet (s) said.

The Curious Little Girl

One afternoon, a little girl named Umm Khalid accompanied her father to visit the Noble Prophet (s). Umm Khalid loved visiting the Prophet's (s) home because he was always so kind and friendly to children. That day, Umm Khalid wore a beautiful yellow dress and had a beaming smile on her face. When the Prophet (s) saw her, he said, "What a beautiful dress!" The Prophet (s) always knew exactly how to make children happy, and Umm Khalid was delighted by his compliment!

As she played in the home, she noticed a birthmark on the Prophet's (s) back. This mark was a sign given to him by Allah. It had previously been revealed that one of the signs of the last Prophet was that he would have such a birthmark on his back!

Umm Khalid was interested in this mark and wanted to look at it more closely. Overcome with curiosity, she reached out to touch the birthmark. When her father saw this, he became embarrassed and quickly pulled her hand away. He did not want his daughter to behave rudely! However, the Prophet (s) was not bothered, and calmed her father down, telling him to let her be. Instead of being upset with her, he let her feel the mark and fulfill her curiosity.

Years later, Umm Khalid still remembered this act of kindness from the Noble Prophet (s) and told others all about his kindness towards her when she was just a child!

Saḥīḥ Bukhārī, Vol. 4, P. 36

Read to Succeed!

◉ During the time of the Prophet (s), women were not respected or appreciated, and were instead looked down upon as unwanted, inferior beings. Some ignorant men even buried their daughters alive when they were babies! By being kind to girls and respecting them, the Prophet (s) taught others to treat their daughters with kindness and fairness. In this story, he praised Umm Khalid's dress and indulged her harmless, childish curiosity.

◉ Once, a man was with the Prophet (s) when he received the news that his wife had given birth to a girl. Hearing this, the man became upset. The Prophet (s) asked, "What happened to make you this upset?"

The man replied, "Never mind, don't worry!" The Prophet (s) insisted on learning what upset the man and asked him yet again. The man sighed and explained, "I have just received terrible news— my wife has delivered a baby girl."

The Prophet (s) responded to the man's ignorant statement wisely, saying, "The earth will support her, the sky will shade her, and Allah will provide her sustenance. She is a beautiful flower for you to enjoy."

◉ When a child was born to Imam as-Sajjad (a), he did not ask, "Is it a boy or a girl?" Instead, his only question was, "Is the child healthy?"

An Accidental Blessing

In the time of the Prophet (s), many people in Medina would bring their newborns to him so he could select virtuous names for them and pray for their wellbeing. It is mustahab to have someone read the adhan and iqaamah into a child's ears right after they are born, and the Prophet (s) was everyone's favorite person to ask this favor from!

People truly loved and respected the Prophet (s), so it was an honor for him to name their children. All parents wanted their children to become familiar with the Prophet's (s) face and voice, and what better time to introduce them than on the day of their birth?

One day, the Prophet (s) gently held a newborn baby, when he suddenly urinated all over the Prophet's (s) clothes! A companion rushed to take the baby out of his hands, but the Prophet (s) shook his head no and told him not to worry. "O Prophet," the companion said, "Don't you want us to take this baby from you? He has ruined your clothes!"

The last thing the Prophet (s) wanted to do was frighten the baby. If they had taken the baby in a rushed and frantic manner, he certainly would have gotten scared and cried! "Don't worry about this," the Prophet calmly told the companion. "Accidents happen. Clothes can easily be washed but it's important not to disturb the child's peace."

The Prophet (s) never mentioned the incident to the child's parents to keep them from feeling embarrassed. He did not want them to feel bad over such a minor accident. Babies cannot control their urges, so this happened often during other naming ceremonies as well. The Prophet (s) was patient and kind, and always knew how to handle the situation to prevent anyone from becoming upset.

Read to Succeed!

- Babies who wet themselves or throw things are not being naughty— they're being babies! As they grow and develop, they learn self control and mature. In this story, the Prophet (s) teaches us that we should not become angry over small, harmless accidents. Think about how bad you might feel if an adult was angry with you over something you could not control! Children are like flowers— they bloom with love and care, but wilt in fear and sadness when spoken to angrily. For this reason, the Prophet (s) never allowed anyone to speak or act harshly with children. His example is always the best for us to learn from!

- When children are crying, we should soothe them quickly and tend to them. The Prophet (s) demonstrated the importance of this once when a baby began crying as he led Salatul Jamaat. The Prophet (s) heard the child's cry and sped up the remainder of the prayer. After the prayer, the Prophet's companions asked, "O Prophet of Allah, why did you recite your prayer faster than normal? Did something happen?" The Prophet (s) replied, "Didn't you hear the baby crying?" He knew the parents must have been praying and needed to quickly attend to the baby's needs.

First Come, First Served

The Noble Prophet (s) loved his daughter Fatimah (a) dearly. Because they both lived in Medina, he was able to visit her often. One day, he went to Fatimah's (a) house to visit with his family. There, Fatimah (a) was cooking while her husband, Imam Ali (a), was taking a nap with their two young sons, Hasan (a) and Husain (a).

As the Noble Prophet sat down to talk to his beloved daughter, Hasan (a) woke up. He was delighted to see his grandfather, the Noble Prophet (s). He ran over to give him a hug. Thirsty after his nap, he asked his grandfather for something to drink.

Sayyidah Fatimah (a) and Imam Ali (a) kept a sheep in their yard. The Prophet (s) took a bowl outside and milked the sheep for Hasan (a). While he was filling the bowl with milk, Hasan's (s) younger brother Husain (s) wandered outside.

When Hasan (s) saw his brother, he smiled. He loved his younger brother very much, so he said to the Prophet (s), "Grandfather, please give the milk to Husain (s) first!"

The Prophet (s) answered kindly, "My dear, how nice of you to think of your brother! Since you asked me first, I will give it to you and you can earn reward by letting you younger brother drink first."

In this moment, the Noble Prophet (s) showed his family just how important it was to respect everyone's rights and not show favoritism. Though it is good to serve younger children first, the Prophet (s) saw this as a good opportunity to teach an important lesson. Our beloved Prophet (s) was fair and kind, and through his example, we can learn how to be fair to others!

Biḥār al-Anwār, Vol. 37, P. 86

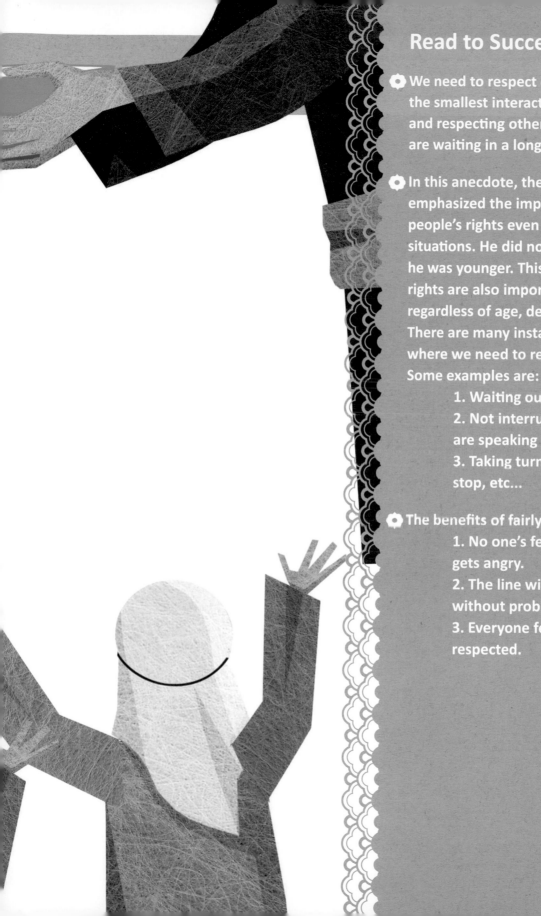

Read to Succeed!

⚙ We need to respect everyone's rights, even in the smallest interactions. After all, taking turns and respecting others is not only for when you are waiting in a long line!

⚙ In this anecdote, the Noble Prophet (s) emphasized the importance of respecting people's rights even in the most innocent of situations. He did not favor Husain (a) because he was younger. This shows us that children's rights are also important, and all people, regardless of age, deserve justice.

There are many instances in our daily lives where we need to respect people's rights. Some examples are:

1. Waiting our turn in line
2. Not interrupting people when they are speaking
3. Taking turns at the playground, bus stop, etc...

⚙ The benefits of fairly taking turns include:

1. No one's feelings are hurt and no one gets angry.
2. The line will move quicker and without problems.
3. Everyone feels like they are being respected.

130

Twenty-One Dates

One day, the Prophet (s) was sitting with his companions outside when a young child approached him. The young boy came close and pleaded, "O Prophet of Allah, please give us something to eat! My sister and I do not have a father, and our mother does not have any money. Please help us, and we will always pray for you!"

The Noble Prophet (s) was an orphan himself, so he knew exactly what kind of hardship these children and their mother must have been going through. He always advised his companions to help orphans and be kind to them whenever possible, for they no longer have parents in the world to look out for them.

The Prophet (s) was impressed with the young orphan's honesty and offer to pray for him. He said, "O son, you speak well! Go to my house and bring whatever food you find." The child set off to do as he was told. When he reached the Prophet's (s) house, the Prophet's (s) wife found dates to give to the child. The boy quickly brought these back to the Prophet (s).

The boy counted exactly twenty-one dates in his hands, and he handed all of them to the Prophet (s). The Prophet (s) looked at the dates and prayed for Allah to bless each of them. Then, turning to the orphan, he said, "O son! Seven dates are for you, seven for your mother, and seven for your sister." The little boy was overjoyed. He smiled and rushed back home to share the dates with his mother and sister.

In those years, Muslims struggled with all kinds of hardship. Twenty-one dates may not sound like much, but they were enough to help a family survive the pangs of hunger.

Majm' Al- Zavāid, Vol. 8, P. 161

Read to Succeed!

- Islam strongly advises us to be kind to orphans. We read in Surah Inshirah, "Never humiliate or bother an orphan." The Noble Prophet (s) said: "Be like a kind father to orphans."

- The Prophet (s) encouraged others to be good, but he always made sure to practice what he preached. In this anecdote, he offered whatever he had in his house to the orphan. He was exactly as kind as he advised his companions to be.

- The Battle of Uhud resulted in the martyrdom of several companions of the Noble Prophet (s). One of the martyrs had a son named Bashir. After the battle, Bashir came to the Prophet (s) to ask, "Where's my father?" The Prophet (s) said, "He has been blessed with martyrdom, may Allah have mercy on him!" Bashir started to cry. The Noble Prophet (s) hugged him and lovingly patted him on his head. Then the Prophet sat the boy next to himself on his mount and comforted him, promising that from then on, he would take care of Bashir as though he was his own son.

- Another important lesson from this story is to cherish our families. We should realize that even if we are safe and comfortable, there are many children in the world who are not. We should help them as much as possible and if we cannot help them, we should remember them in our prayers.

A Beautiful Name

One of the companions of the Noble Prophet (s) was a pious and hardworking man from Africa. He was a very good man, but the people used to taunt him because of the color of his skin, calling him Aswad, which means black in Arabic. Aswad didn't like that people only focused on the color of his skin, rather than his personality.

The Prophet (s) too, did not like that the people did this. The Prophet (s) knew that what makes a person special is their personality, good deeds, and actions. So, he decided to change this nickname and call him Abyaz, which in Arabic means bright. This name suits a person who has a *noorani*, or bright, face both in this world and the hereafter. This name reflected his personality and traits, like his obedience to Allah!

From that day onwards, people started using his new name in respect for the Noble Prophet (s). Abyaz was delighted at what the Noble Prophet (s) had done. He felt relieved and happy.

Read to Succeed!

❋ The Noble Prophet's (s) kindness and love was not limited to the rich, influential, and powerful; rather it was felt by everyone equally, as seen in this anecdote.

❋ If the Noble Prophet (s) saw a Muslim with a name that did not suit him, he encouraged others to call them by a different one. Once, he asked a man what his name was. The man answered his name was Bagheez, which in Arabic means 'one who is revengeful'. The Prophet (s) changed his name and said, "You are Habib meaning friend, from now on." Another time, a woman came to the Prophet (s) and he asked her name. "Aasi" (a word that means 'female rebel'), she replied. The Noble Prophet (s) changed her name to 'Jameelah', which means 'beautiful woman'. Giving people beautiful names was a tradition of the Prophet (s).

❋ The Ahlul Bayt (a) have advised people to choose noble names for their children. The names Muhammad, Ali, Fatimah, Hasan, Husain, Ja'far, and Musa are the seven heavenly names that are recommended.

Don't Throw Stones, Dear Son

The city of Medina is an oasis famous for its date trees. Orchards full of date trees can be found all over the city! One particularly tall date palm towered over a young boy's house, and he often helped himself to its dates.

He would usually throw stones at the dates to make them fall to the ground. The date palm belonged to a landowner in Medina, so every time the boy plucked a date, he was technically stealing from the landowner!

Dates often fell from the palm trees on their own, so it was not uncommon to find dates of all shapes and sizes on the ground in orchards. The boy could have easily taken those fallen dates to eat instead, and the owner would not have minded. Throwing stones at the tree, however, damaged the leaves and also knocked unripe dates to the ground. By taking directly from the tree, the boy was causing harm to the tree *and* stealing!

One day, the owner saw the boy throw stones at his tree. He was angry and upset to see his tree being damaged, but knew he should not speak to the boy with anger.

He approached the boy and asked him patiently if he would join him to go speak to Prophet Muhammad (s). The tree owner thought the Prophet (s) could handle the situation better, as he was the best example of kindness.

When they went to see the Prophet (s), the owner explained the situation to him. The Prophet (s) then kindly asked the boy, "Dear son, why do you pelt stones at that tree?"

The boy replied, "I throw stones to hit the dates and make them fall! Once they fall, I gather them and eat them."

The Prophet (s) asked, "Did you realize that your actions actually harm the date tree? By throwing stones, you are ripping its leaves and making holes in the trunk! Your stones could also hurt you or another person nearby."

The boy shook his head. "Wow," he said with surprise, "I had no idea! I feel terrible for doing that now!"

The Prophet gently told him, "Don't throw stones at the tree. Instead, why don't you gather the dates that have already fallen to the ground?"

As the boy continued to apologize, the Prophet (s) reached out and gently patted his head. The tree owner was relieved that the problem had been solved without any arguing or yelling! That day, Prophet Muhammad (s) showed him that kindness truly is the best way to solve a problem.

Ḥikāyatnāmeh Payāmbar, Vol. 8, P. 22

Read to Succeed!

- If someone makes a mistake and we want to correct them, it must be done with kindness. When dealing with children in particular, we must be very patient and kind, just as the Prophet (s) was in this anecdote.

- In a Quranic example, Allah asked Prophet Musa (a) and Prophet Haroon (a) to behave kindly even to an opressor. Verses 43-44 of Surah Taha say, "Go to the Pharaoh because he has rebelled, and speak softly to him. Maybe he will accept or fear Allah!"

- Kids have the right to play and enjoy themselves, but not at the cost of harming someone else. The Prophet (s) never objected to children playing, but this anecdote shows that a child's behavior must not harm another person or their property.

Bravo, Imam Husain (a)!

Imam Hasan (a) and Imam Husain (a) often wrestled with one another while growing up, and both children always wanted to win. Though they knew it was only a game, they played it with seriousness and dedication.

Both children were under eight years old, but wrestled like professionals! Their father, Imam Ali (a) was known for his strength and bravery, so it was no surprise that his sons could wrestle so well.

Their parents never objected to their wrestling, because they knew that these kinds of games are good for children. Games that keep kids physically active help them grow stronger and more brave!

One day, Imam Hasan (a) and Imam Husain (a) wrestled in front of their grandfather, the Noble Prophet (s), who watched their match very closely. During the match, he rooted for Imam Hasan (a), and said, "O Hasan, O Hasan, catch your brother Husain!"

Imam Hasan (a), thanks to the Prophet's (s) encouragement, gained energy and fought better than ever before.

Sayyidah Fatimah (a) was watching curiously. She wondered why the Noble Prophet (s) was cheering only for Imam Hasan (a), who was older, instead of the younger Imam Husain (a), knowing that younger kids usually need more encouragement?

She asked her father, "O dearest father! Are you cheering for Hasan (a)?"

The Prophet smiled and answered, "My daughter, Angel Jibraeel is also here — and he is rooting for Husain (a)!

Sayyidah Fatimah (a) smiled with understanding. Husain (a) was not alone as she thought, and he had encouragement from an angel of Allah!

Read to Succeed!

- The Noble Prophet (s) encouraged children's games that were competitive in nature, because such games taught children how to win and lose.

- Sometimes, he himself started games among kids. For example, he once made his young grand-children stand in a line and said, "Whoever reaches me first will get a prize." They happily took part in the race trying hard to outdo one another. When they reached the Prophet (s) they jumped into his arms while he hugged and kissed them affectionately.

Biḥār al-Anwār, Vol. 42, P. 276, 262, 265 & 291

Where's Your Nightingale?

Young Abu Umayr loved his pet nightingale. His nightingale was a beautiful bird, and it chirped beautiful songs. Abu Umayr and his nightingale were the best of friends. When he spoke to his nightingale, he really felt that the nightingale actually understood what he was saying.

After some time, the nightingale suddenly became sick. It stopped flying and singing, and was too weak and frail. Abu Umayr was very upset to see this, but there was nothing he could do! Within days, his beautiful bird passed away.

Abu Umayr was sad and missed his nightingale very much. He didn't feel like going out and playing with his friends anymore, and instead stayed quietly at home.

One day, the Prophet (s) saw him and noticed that he appeared unhappy. He asked one of his friends if they knew the reason for his sadness. They told the Prophet that he was sad because his bird had died.

Seeing someone sad, especially a child, was very difficult for the Prophet (s). Whenever he saw someone sad, he tried his best to make them happy. The Prophet (s) went to Abu Umayr, looked at him and gently asked him, "Dear Abu Umayr, what happened to *Nughair*[1]?"

With this gentle question, the Prophet (s) expressed his condolences. Realizing that the Prophet (s) cared and shared his grief, Abu Umayr felt comforted. The Prophet smiled at the young boy, and Abu Umayr gave him a smile back.

1.Nughair is the Arabic for nightingale

Imtā' Al- Asmā', Vol. 2, P. 196

Read to Succeed!

In this story we see how important it was to the Noble Prophet (s) to relieve other people from their sadness. One day when Allah's Messenger (s) was returning home from the market, he saw a slave girl sitting on the pathway, crying. The Prophet (s) asked why she was crying. "O Prophet of Allah! I'm late and afraid of being punished," she said. "Walk ahead of me and show me your master's house," said the Prophet (s). When they reached the place, the Noble Prophet (s) stood by the door and greeted the members of the house, but no one answered. He greeted them again but still no response came. He repeated his greeting and this time they came out to say, "Peace be on you O Prophet of Allah!" The Prophet (s) asked, "Is there a reason why you didn't answer the first two times?" They responded, "O Prophet of Allah! When we heard your heavenly voice, we wanted to hear it again and again." The Prophet (s) said, "This slave girl is late. Please do not punish her." They said, "O Prophet of Allah, with the blessing of your arrival, we will free this girl!"

Love Children Fairly

One day, the Noble Prophet (s) was sitting with his companions in the masjid when a young boy entered the building. The child saw his father seated near the Prophet (s) and ran toward him. The father smiled at his son, and pulled him into his lap. He caressed the child's head gently and continued listening to the Prophet (s) speak.

A little while later, the man's young daughter also entered the masjid and ran over to him. He smiled at her as well, and reached out to smooth back her hair. However, instead of pulling her into his lap, he seated her on the floor next to him. The girl was happy to have received her father's attention and did not think much about where he seated her. She was too busy looking around the masjid to notice!

The Noble Prophet (s) noticed the way this father interacted with his children. He was pleased to see him treat both of his children with love and affection, but knew there was always room to do even better.

He suggested to this father, "Brother, perhaps it would have been even better to pull both of your children into your lap instead of just one. Even if they are too young to notice, this is a good way to make sure they both feel equally loved by you!"

The man was amazed at what the Prophet (s) had said. SubhaanAllah! Islam protected the rights of children in even the smallest of ways! He understood that he should have either held both children in his lap, or seated both next to him.

The man looked down at his two children and realized how important it was to be aware of even the little things. He ruffled the hair of both children with affection, and pulled his daughter into his lap, too. Now, both children were treated like equals. His daughter was especially happy to be in the warmth of her father's arms!

The Prophet (s) nodded approvingly and said to the man, "Now you have ordained justice."

Ḥikāyatnāmeh Payāmbar, Vol. 7, P. 308

Read to Succeed!

◉ Parents should treat their children fairly, and shouldn't play favorites. The Noble Prophet (s) said, "Allah wants you to treat your children justly, even when it comes to kissing them." Once, a man kissed one of his children, but not the other. The Noble Prophet (s) asked him kindly, "Brother, why didn't you kiss both of your dear children? Kiss both, so both will feel the love you have for them!"

◉ Bashir was a companion of the Noble Prophet (s). One day, he came to the Noble Prophet (s) and said, "O Prophet of Allah! I want to gift a part of my property to one of my sons." "Have you gifted the rest of your children in the same way?" inquired the Prophet (s). "No," replied Bashir. The Prophet of Allah gently advised him, "My friend, do your best to be fair to both of your children! Give each an equal share of your property."

Showing Children Love

The Prophet (s) loved his grandsons, Imam Hasan (a) and Imam Husain (a) very much. Whenever he saw them, he was filled with joy and showered them with kisses.

A man once saw the Prophet (s) hugging and kissing his grandchildren, and said to the Prophet (s) "I have ten children, but I've never kissed any of them." The Prophet (s) was very sad to hear this. His heart sank for this man's children, because they were being deprived of their father's love.

The Prophet (s) said to him, "Whoever is not kind or loving to children will be deprived of Allah's mercy. Indeed, the best way to receive His mercy is by showing mercy!"

Biḥār al-Anwār, Vol. 43, P. 282

Read to Succeed!

⚙ The Noble Prophet (s) said, "Whoever kisses his child earns a reward with Allah, and he who makes his child happy will be made happy by Allah on the Day of Judgement."

⚙ The Prophet (s) showed affection to Hasan (a) and Husain (a) in many different ways. He played with them, fed them with his own hands, carried them on his back, and even gave rides to them.

A Kind Grandfather

Imam Hasan (a) and Imam Husain (a) loved to play with their grandfather. Whenever he visited them, they would both climb onto his back. They were both too young for camel and horse riding, so they practiced riding on their grandfather's back instead. Prophet Muhammad (s) would always play along, and truly loved to entertain them.

Whenever they rode on him, they actually felt like they were real riders. They would call out loudly, "Go! Go! Go!" The Prophet (s) would carry them from one end of the room to the other and happily exclaim, "What a good camel you two have, and what great riders you are!"

One day, Imam Husain (a) was with the Prophet (s) while he was leading a large group of people in prayer.

When the Prophet (s) went down in sajdah, Imam Husain (a) moved closer and climbed up on the Prophet's (s) back, crying out as he would when playing with him, "Go! Go! Go!"

Prophet Muhammad (s) wasn't upset at all. He knew Imam Husain (a) was just playing and being a kid.

The Prophet (s) continued his prayer. While rising up, however, he was careful to move slowly so Imam Husain (a) did not fall or hurt himself. Imam Husain (a) climbed up on the Prophet's (s) back several times during prayer and continued playing with him, and the Prophet (s) remained focused and careful at the same time.